Heart Prints

♥

The Power of Making Connections in the Classroom and Beyond

ANNE SCHOBER

A Collection of Stories from a Freedom Writer Teacher and her Students

Forward by Erin Gruwell

LIBRARY TALES PUBLISHING

Published by Library Tales Publishing, Inc.
www.LibraryTalesPublishing.com
www.Facebook.com/LibraryTalesPublishing

Copyright © 2014 by Anne Schober

No part of this publication may be reproduced, stored in a retrieval system, or transmitted in any form or by any means, electronic, mechanical, photocopying, recording, scanning, or otherwise, except as permitted under Sections 107 or 108 of the 1976 United States Copyright Act, without the prior written permission of the Publisher.

Trademarks: Library Tales Publishing, Library Tales, the Library Tales Publishing logo, and related trade dress are trademarks or registered trademarks of Library Tales Publishing, Inc. and/or its affiliates in the United States and other countries, and may not be used without written permission. All other trademarks are the property of their respective owners.

For general information on our other products and services, please contact our Customer Care Department at 1-800-754-5016, or fax 917-463-0892. For technical support, please e-mail Office@Librarytales.com

Library Tales Publishing also publishes its books in a variety of electronic formats. Every content that appears in print is available in electronic books.

ISBN-13: 978-0692204092
ISBN-10: 0692204091

*For Michael, Michelle, JoAnne and Stephen...
My reasons for believing that dreams really do come true.*

Acknowledgements

Heart Prints is the final product of many years of life lessons and stories learned along the way. It is a book of heartbreak, hope, loss, laughter and joy. It is filled with stories from my students, some from long ago and some recently graduated. One of my golden rules as a teacher was to always respect my students writing and to maintain their voice in all of their writing pieces. I continued that philosophy while writing *Heart Prints*. I have not changed my students writing in any way. What is printed is what was sent to me. Their words are golden; their voices are sincere. While there may be some grammatical errors found within their powerful words, I believe their message was stronger when left intact. They took a chance by sharing their stories not only with me, but with the world. *David, Erin, Patrick, Rosa, Maura, Matt, Katie, Ivory, Bridgette, Abbey, Kayla, EB, Lindsey, Johnston, Adam, Emily, Anita, Michael, Stephen, JoAnne, Michelle and Monica* ...thank you for being a part of my life and allowing me to be a part of yours.

Sue, Jim, and Leslie... Thank you for always supporting me and being my biggest cheerleaders! Your presence in my life has been a constant source of light, love and inspiration.

Dad... You are a beacon of strength, faith, love and courage. Through all the heartache you have endured, your constant daily struggle with pain, and your perseverance to never give up while fighting cancer are inspirational to all who know you. Thank you for believing in me and for loving me unconditionally. You are my hero.

Mom... You were my angel on earth and now you are my special angel in heaven. Twenty years have passed and it feels like yesterday. I can still see your sparkling eyes, hear your contagious chuckle, smell your Clinque perfume, and feel your warm hugs. I am honored to live my life as you did... cherishing each and every moment. I miss you more today than yesterday ... you are "the wind beneath my wings".

Erin, the Freedom Writers and the Freedom Writer teachers... You have inspired me to be the teacher and person I am. You taught me to teach with my heart, listen with my heart, and love unconditionally. Your support and guidance have been unconditional, constant and strong. I am blessed to have over 350 people I call my family. And to the July 2007 crew... you are my heart and soul and I am honored to know and love each of you. Thank you for allowing me to share my story for the first time with all of you... you are my heroes.

Sister Eileen McGuigan... When I was in high school, academics were second to boys and all things social. I barely passed my math classes and many times would skip gym so that I could spend time with my friends instead. I struggled not because I was a bad student but because I didn't feel that anything I was learning was going to help me in my future.

But, all that changed when I walked into your English class. You took the time to know your students and encouraged us to work to our fullest potential. You taught me the skills I needed to write a well-organized paper while also teaching me the importance of using my voice to share my stories with the world. You taught me to write with courage. You were the first person to recognize that I became alive while I was writing. Thank you for believing in me.

Carol and Patrick... Thank you for taking the time to read my story, offering your feedback and directing me toward this finished product. I can never thank you enough for your confidence and time.

Greg... Thank you for sharing your artistic talents. You have a gift that the world needs to see... Keep creating and sharing your skills for all to appreciate.

Denise and Denny ... Thank you for being more than a brother and sister to me. You are the ears, shoulders, and hearts I have needed throughout my life. You have been my constant in a sometimes confusing world. Thank you for teaching me that life is a fun adventure when spent with those you are proud to call your friends.

Michelle, JoAnne and Stephen... You are my gifts from God and because of you I have become a better person. Each of you is unique and yet the perfect combination of love, honesty, strength, hope and laughter. You make my heart smile as I continue to watch you grow into the most amazing young people that I knew you would be. You are my angels.

Michael... My best friend and the love of my life. Thank you for believing in me and pushing me to write my story. You have been the one constant in my life and, through the good times and the bad, our love has become stronger and stronger. Twenty eight years ago I became your wife. Twenty eight years later, I feel like I am still on my honeymoon. Thank you for being mine. Thank you for being my everything. *More.*

Foreword
By Erin Gruwell

As an ordinary teacher who has had extraordinary "students," I have learned that everyone has a story. I began my career in teaching unruly teens who eventually became accomplished story-tellers, known as the Freedom Writers. I then progressed to teaching dedicated teachers, affectionately dubbed Freedom Writer Teachers, who also have a story to share.

Even though I was the one standing in the front of a classroom, I was humbled by the lessons I learned from both sets of "students" sitting before me. These lessons turned into powerful stories—stories that couldn't be contained in a classroom, nor a school or even a community. These stories -- whether written by an insecure teenager trying to find his or her voice, or passionate teachers, trying to hone theirs – riveted their readers.

Just as the Freedom Writers penned *The Freedom Writers Diary,* the Freedom Writer Teachers followed suit by penning *Teaching Hope* — both best sellers, respectively. What resonated with the authors of both compilations of short stories was that writing is a cathartic journey of exploration. For some, the writing process opened Pandora's Box, but before the writer could uncover hope, they first felt pain. After all, their story was now on paper—for them to be judged, evaluated, and forced to relive memories.

Although both the Freedom Writers and the Freedom Writer Teachers wrote and published their stories anonymously - reflecting on the power of universal truths by holding a mirror up to their own lives - many of the authors have chosen to step out of the shadows and own their stories. Anne Schober is one of those courageous storytellers who chose not to be cloaked in secrecy or hide behind the number on a page. She made the leap from paper to advocate, by using her own story to encourage her students and her readers to tell their own.

Embarrassingly, I almost did not give Anne the chance to share her story with the Freedom Writers and me. In a twist of fate, I judged Anne - just as the Freedom Writers originally judged me for my polka dots and pearls, and my perceived "white privilege." Anne applied to be a Freedom Writer Teacher—an educational opportunity we've bestowed on teachers across the globe that come to Long Beach, California and are exposed to the ingredients in our "secret sauce." As we selected scholarship recipients, we assumed that the only teachers that would be able to successfully tackle the taboos of *The Freedom Writers Diary* would be those who taught in tough inner-city schools. Leading up to giving away these coveted spots, the Freedom Writers and I faced battles with conservative shock jocks blasting our book on radio shows, unreasonable school boards trying to ban the book from their schools and members of the Ku Klux Klan. Our book had been called "pornography" by nay-sayers, and the teachers who dared teach it without permission would be stepping on landmines of profanity or perpetrators. I assumed that teachers brave enough to teach our book would sneak it into their classroom like contraband and wave it before gang members like the Holy Grail.

The lessons I taught in Room 203 had academic merit. After visiting many schools around the country, I became humbled and exhilarated by teachers who were using *The Freedom Writers Diary* in their classrooms. With the Freedom Writers help, I began to assemble teachers from around the world. We were resolute that our recruits had to believe that when it came to teaching, one size does not fit all; and above all else, these teachers had to be willing to teach to a kid and not to a test.

When Anne Schober applied, I immediately passed on her application. She was a former beauty queen teaching in a Catholic school. Her school was closer to the Amish country than the mean streets of Philly. Every stereotype imaginable came to mind when it came to this red headed lass teaching in a parochial school. I falsely envisioned nuns cracking the knuckles of any teen who dared to pick up our book. Luckily, I was wrong.

In typical Anne fashion, she was not going to let statistics or stereotypes of her application allow us to judge her unwillingly. Even though Anne taught in a Catholic, private school, she wanted to prove that we would not be setting her up for failure. She loaded up her students in a caravan, and drove to an event where I was speaking at in New Jersey. She was determined to let me see beyond her red hair and freckles in person. Yes, she was what my students dubbed, "a nice white lady." Yes, she taught at a Catholic school. Yes, her community was more rural than urban. But stereotypes immediately flew out the window. She let me know that her kids had a story. That she, too, had a story. And together, their story had to be told.

So I capitulated. Willing so. And have I never looked back. Because the Anne that stood before me, pleading her case, has been pleading the case of others ever since.

I took a chance and flew Anne to Long Beach where she learned techniques directly from the Freedom Writers and me. She went back to her classroom and created magic in the form of her own group of Freedom Writers known as "The Mix." Her and her posse's successes were more than any of us could have imagined.

Anne believes in each student, she believes that each student has a story, and she does everything she can to teach each student what he or she needs to know to succeed. Anne exudes an energy that needs to be bottled up and sprinkled over every teacher in every school district. With her students following the mantra "Be the change you wish to see in the world," The Mix set out to help others who sometimes felt neglected, overlooked, and invisible, much like themselves. They helped to rebuild New Orleans, remodeled a school in Nashville and built them a playground, but, more importantly, changed the environment of their own school. The kids who were once looked at as "stupid "or "hopeless," transformed into the rock stars of her school. They created a legacy that none of us thought possible.

The Mix graduated and Anne continued to em-

-power her students to change the world. Her students wrote a book, helped at a local orphanage, and created a safe haven for teens called Building Hope. Her students learned firsthand the power of acceptance, tolerance and the importance of connecting with one another in order to form a family. Needless to say, when Anne told me she was leaving her school, I assured her that she would still be a teacher—she would be teaching on a much larger platform. Her memoir, *Heart Prints* would give her a platform to do so.

Through the years, consisting of several school visits, many home cooked meals and meetings in states far and wide, I have had the privilege of seeing Anne's students go from squirrely freshman to distinguished graduates. I have watched her own children pursue their dreams, I have reveled in her father watching his own daughter find the courage to bear witness to her painful story and begin the healing process. And most impressively, I have cheered as Anne has followed a higher calling. She has morphed from simply my "student" into my teacher, a beloved friend and a close confidant.

What follows is Anne's journey in the classroom and her transformation from a teacher to a Freedom Writer Teacher. Along the way, she encountered many triumphs as well as a few obstacles, but, through it all, her students learned about life and she learned about them. She learned to connect with her students on a level that surprised even her. She created a safe environment where her students felt at home. She opened herself up to her students so that they would open their hearts to her and their peers.

Introduction

Step to the line if you have ever had braces.
Step to the line if you live with only one parent.
Step to the line if you know someone who is addicted to drugs.
Step to the line if you have ever heard a gunshot.
Step to the line if you know someone who was raped.
Step to the line if you know someone who lost their life to gang violence.
Step to the line if you are scared to go home.

With a piece of tape down the middle of the classroom and students lined up on either side, what began as a "game" slowly became a glimpse into the lives of my students. For each question asked, for each foot that stepped on the line, I was methodically ripping apart the layers of each student. Slowly they revealed themselves to each other by comparing battle wounds, to see who else had experienced the same as they had and to allow others to see who they really were. In reality, we were forming an important element needed in the classroom.... we were forming a family by making connections.

While they were actively participating in this "game", I was taking mental notes on each of my new family members. Seventeen students had no father. Twenty eight students had been sexually abused. Ten students had at least one parent in jail. Thirty students had come to school hungry.

Ninety students knew where to buy drugs and forty five students knew someone who suffered from an addiction. Tears enveloped my heart. How was I to begin to teach a lesson on grammar, research skills, Hemingway or O'Brien when I knew that sitting in front of me were victims of physical, verbal and sexual abuse, survivors and victims of the street, hungry teens who had not eaten in days, young parents who had not slept because their baby needed their attention, sons and daughters who had never met their father because he was in jail or was killed when they were younger? These were my students and they were the reasons I came to school every day, ready to give a warm hug, lend a listening ear or a few dollars for lunch. I saw each of my students as the future. Whether they had a learning disability or were a strong honors student, I believed that each of my students had the capacity to change the world. All they needed was to find the confidence within themselves to believe what I witnessed through their words, actions, and even their struggles. I was their cheerleader and, for many, I was their mom away from home.

And yet, after thirteen years in the classroom, I left. Why did I leave? Was I burnt out? The answer is complicated, yet easy. It was time. It was time to focus on what I knew needed my full attention, my own family. Teaching took over my life. I would grade in the car while going away for a weekend, taking away time from my husband and kids. I would grade during Notre Dame Football games, which is sacrilegious in my world. I would work on lesson plans while eating dinner. I would not accept social invitations because I knew I had too much work to do for school. I placed school first, family second, and that is something I regret still to this day. It took a big "slap in the face" for reality to set in; a sting that continues to hurt but has slowly healed over time. The wakeup call I received caused me to take notice to what was slipping away right in front of my eyes, and I was oblivious because school had become my world. I left teaching because it was time.

Leaving the classroom was emotional. I was going to miss my connections with the students. I was going to miss the peers who supported me. I was going to miss my room, my safe haven for many, many years. I was going to miss my identity. On my last day, I felt alone. I knew that once I locked my door, I would never be back. I would be turning my classroom over to a new, younger teacher who would be teaching the kids that would have been mine. I knew that my life as a teacher was to be no more, and the search for my new identity would just be beginning.

One of the hardest moments I had to face when I made the decision to leave the classroom was to tell Erin Gruwell, the founder of the Freedom Writer Foundation, but more importantly, my inspiration, soul-sister, and hero. I felt I was letting her down. She believed in me. She trained me to be the best teacher possible, and I was leaving the battleground. As I talked to her on the phone, my heart was pounding and the tears were flowing. Her words were encouraging and directed me toward happiness and acceptance.

"Anne, you are not leaving teaching because the world is your classroom," Erin said. "Your future is filled with unlimited possibilities. But, I am going to challenge you to do one thing for me."

"Okay," I said uncertainly.

"I want you to write a book about you, your

teaching experiences, your life in the classroom, or whatever you wish to write about. I challenge you to write a book. You have a story that needs to be told."

Writing my story was difficult because it was not just *my* story. My family, my students, and my fellow teachers became an integral part of my every day. Our lives were so intertwined and connected that it was impossible to separate the two. And so what follows is that story, *our* story. After I became a Freedom Writer teacher, my life as a teacher changed beyond words. I learned from Erin Gruwell how to teach with my heart so that the rest will follow. This book encourages teachers to open their hearts and their eyes to the students in each of their classrooms. This book exposes the realities of the classroom when a teacher realizes that each person has a story to tell and each person has a voice that needs to be heard. This book is a story of connections, success, heartbreak and love. This book is an impassioned call to learn to teach, love and speak with your heart and your life will never be the same. Welcome to *Heart Prints*... welcome to our world!

Anne Schober

Part One
The Back Story…

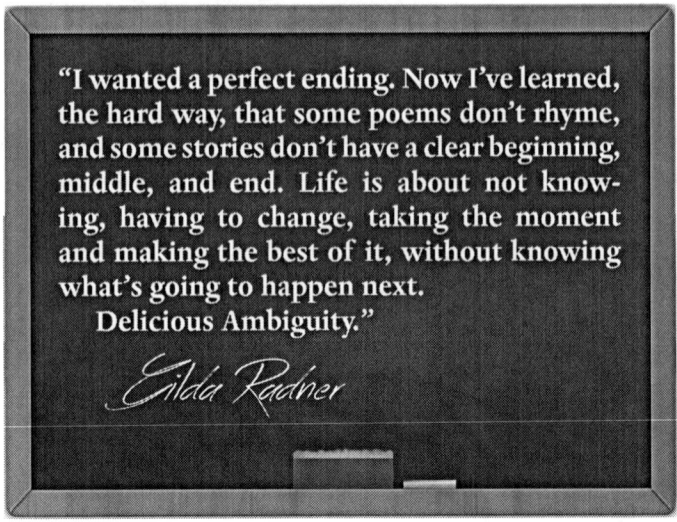

"I wanted a perfect ending. Now I've learned, the hard way, that some poems don't rhyme, and some stories don't have a clear beginning, middle, and end. Life is about not knowing, having to change, taking the moment and making the best of it, without knowing what's going to happen next.
Delicious Ambiguity."

Gilda Radner

I used to perform autopsies.

So, how did I become a teacher? How did I go from dead bodies to a group of living, breathing (sometimes awake) students? The leap was slow, but the final landing place was worth the journey. I know that memoirs are meant to focus on one theme, event and/or moment, and this book will do so, but sometimes it is important to know the back story before you can begin to understand the present.

When I was a senior in high school, I had no idea what I wanted to be; but, I did know that I wanted to go to college and experience all that it had to offer. The majority of my family was involved in the medical field in some capacity, and, since I had no real direction, I thought that this was something I should look into. After researching different fields, I settled on exploring the field of Radiologic Technology. This type of major was not predominately found in the college setting but rather in the hospital classroom. However, Gannon University, located in Erie, PA, offered this major and my mom and I set off to visit the school six hours away from home. After a weekend of tours and lots of snow, I knew that this was my school of choice.

In August of 1981, I traveled to Erie, unpacked my bags and began a two year experience that would change my life forever. Having freedom to do what I wanted, when I wanted, was overwhelming. I went to every party I could, where I partied, partied, and partied some more. Attending class was secondary. When I did go to class, I was overwhelmed by the amount of information with which I was confronted. Medical terms. Chemistry facts. Human body dissection. I found it was easier to skip class than be confronted with information that just did not make sense to me. I was beginning my downward spiral. Little did I know that one event would take me to a dark abyss.

It was a Friday night and I was getting ready to go to another frat party with a group of my friends. I put on a pair of jeans, a sweatshirt and pulled my hair back into a high pony tail. Being a bit overweight, I felt I looked "cute", which was all I was trying to achieve. We arrived at the party, paid our admission fee, and my friends and I headed to the basement where the music was blaring and the beer was flowing. The smell of sweat, lust and alcohol was overwhelming, but it made the ambiance that much more enticing. My friends were slowly being picked up, one by one being hit on by cute guys who asked them to dance. Eventually, I was found to be all alone. This was typical – just me and my glass of beer, dancing together. Out of the corner of my eye, I made eye contact with a really cute blonde guy who began to make his way toward me. I felt my heart beating a bit faster as I was sure he was not going to talk to me, but I wished I was wrong. As he approached, I realized his eyes were set on me. He grabbed my cup, filled it with more beer, and began making small talk. "What's your name?" "Where are you from?" "What's your major?" I was in awe. This older, handsome college student was talking to me, an overweight freshman who was simply a wallflower. As he continued to engage me in conversation, he simultaneously refilled my beer. I could feel myself slowly becoming more unstable, the alcohol taking effect. The next question I can remember I will never forget: "Would you like a tour of the frat house?" How could I refuse? This very good-looking older college frat brother was interested in me! So, of course, I followed. He grabbed my hand as we climbed the stairs. We walked through the kitchen, past the living room and up another two flight of stairs. "Aren't you giving me a tour of the house? You've missed a lot of rooms!" His words were eerily prophetic, "There is only one room that I want to show you." With those words, my confidence slowly melted away, but I followed anyway.

What happened next is not something that is easy to write about, nor is it something that is easy to share; however, this lone event changed who I was and made me who I am today.

We approached a bedroom on the fourth floor of the frat house. It was secluded, dark, and small. He closed the door behind me, locked it, and filled my empty beer glass with Jack Daniels. He took his hand and forced the alcohol into my mouth while telling me to "drink, it will help me to relax." I began shaking as he grabbed my glass and shoved me onto the bed. The music was blaring, Queen's

Bohemian Rhapsody hauntingly echoing my thoughts as my mind tried to wrap around the reality of what was happening. His power encompassed my weakened strength. As he grabbed my arms, I lost hope. I screamed; he turned the music up louder. I tried to get away; he fought me harder. I cried as he ripped off my sweatshirt and jeans; determined to finish what he intended to do. Through my screams, my tears, my determination to free myself, he raped me. He stole my innocence. He took away my confidence. He took me and I have never fully recovered.

Realizing he had passed out, I grabbed my ripped clothes, hurriedly got dressed, ran out of the house and made my way back to the dorm. Recognizing I lost my dorm keys, I began pounding on the door to my room. There was no answer. Where were my friends? Why did they leave me there? Why didn't they come looking for me? I ran to the bathroom, showered, trying to remove the filth that covered my body. I felt dirty. I was scared, scarred, and broken. I was alone.

Days passed and my friends noticed that I was withdrawn, different, and quiet. I should have told them, but I didn't. I kept this horrible secret to myself and, in turn, began drinking more and more and eating less and less. Over the next two months I lost over 50 pounds, my diet consisting of Jack Daniels and cigarettes. I continued to go to frat parties, but I never returned to that frat house where my life was forever changed. However, my time in class was non-existent and my GPA became horrendous. I knew I needed help, but I kept my pain and secret to myself. One night, after a drunken binge, I was found passed out in downtown Erie. My parents received word that I was "ill" and put me on a plane to fly home.

I don't remember much about my homecoming, but I do remember the doctor appointments, all of them saying I was "fine" after each test came back normal. When asked if I would speak to a psychologist, I agreed, but again kept my secret mine. No one was going to find out what happened that night. Instead, I "made up" what I thought the doctor wanted to hear: "I miss home". "School is just really hard."

"I don't really have any friends". After all the tests, doctors, and consults, my diagnosis was "cluster headaches" and I was sent back to Erie with medicine. Again, I was alone with my secret.

Upon my return, I was asked to meet with my advisor who proceeded to tell me that I could no longer continue at Gannon. My GPA was a 0.8 and the University did not think there was any way I was going to rebound from my dismal academic record. With much pleading from myself and my parents, I was given a second chance. I enrolled in a different major, Medical Assistant, moved into an off-campus efficiency apartment, and tried to get myself together. Living alone, only blocks from where I was raped, tore at my soul. I faced those horrible memories and demons every single day. It was made worse when I heard that six other young women were raped by the same person, in the same house, but again, I kept silent. Instead, I became immersed in my studies and, after 21 months, my parents came to celebrate my graduation. My empty diploma case in hand, proud smiles gracing every picture, I still had one more hurdle to conquer.

My internship was beginning the following week and, as my parents left, I was left alone, again, my secret becoming harder to control. I felt hopeless, scared and uncertain of my future. The money my parents sent me went directly to alcohol instead of to school to pay for my internship. I still went to the hospital, cared for the patients while being hung over and hurting, and completed my required hours; however, when it came time to receive my diploma, I knew it would be impossible because I had never paid the tuition bill. I left Erie without my diploma and came home to an uncertain future with my secret haunting my dreams.

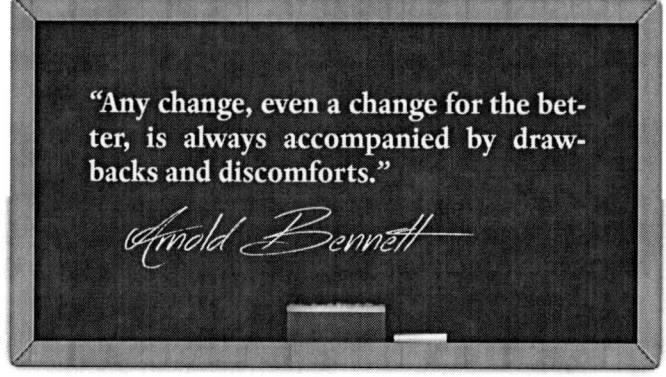

"Any change, even a change for the better, is always accompanied by drawbacks and discomforts."
Arnold Bennett

Finding a job was easy. It's funny, nobody asked to see a diploma; they simply checked my transcripts and grades. My Medical Assistant GPA was something I was very proud; I received a 3.8, and proudly flaunted my achievement. I interviewed at a local Community Osteopathic Hospital and was offered a job as a Unit Clerk. I loved working with the nurses and the doctors and eventually, when a position opened in Pathology for a Medical Secretary, I applied and accepted this challenging position. Working in the "basement" was interesting and intriguing. One day I would type frozen section results, and the next I would be looking at amputated legs. A few months into my new position,

I received a phone call from my boss, a wonderfully intelligent yet goofy Pathologist, asking me if I would help to assist him with an autopsy since the regular assistant was away. With a payment of $10 per body, I knew this was an opportunity I did not want to miss, so I happily agreed.

Walking into the autopsy room was frightening. The Pathologist had not yet arrived, so I was left alone in the sterile room. To my left were instruments of every size and shape hanging obtrusively from the ceiling. To my right were rows of shelves that housed jars holding amputated feet and hands, fetuses, bunions and even objects that had been removed from different bodily orifices. In front of me an elderly woman was lying cold and lifeless on the stainless steel table. Many thoughts were running through my head and I was grateful when the doctor finally arrived. He saved me from my overactive imagination. Sensing my nerves, he proceeded to pull out a saw and turned it on, the sound piercing my ears. Instead of beginning the dissection, the doctor proceeded to chase me around the room, and when he finally caught up to me, he placed the saw on my arm. I screamed. I ran. I tried to escape his evil antics. As I glanced back, I realized the Pathologist was laughing hysterically. It turned out that the saw does not penetrate skin, only bone. And with this small joke, I was christened into the world of being an autopsy assistant.

I am sure that every Pathologist has his/her own routine, and what I witnessed that day was something I will never forget. He began with the head, making a precise slice at the hairline so that the skin could be pulled down without harming the face. After cutting through the skull and removing the brain, he proceeded throughout the rest of the body, removing organs, weighing each as they were detached, examining with exactness, while searching for the cause of death. My job was to weigh, remove and cut whatever he asked, and drain the blood to try and keep the body clean. After several hours, the autopsy was complete. My final job was to place all the organs into a bag then back into the body, and finally sew the body back together. My first autopsy was complete.

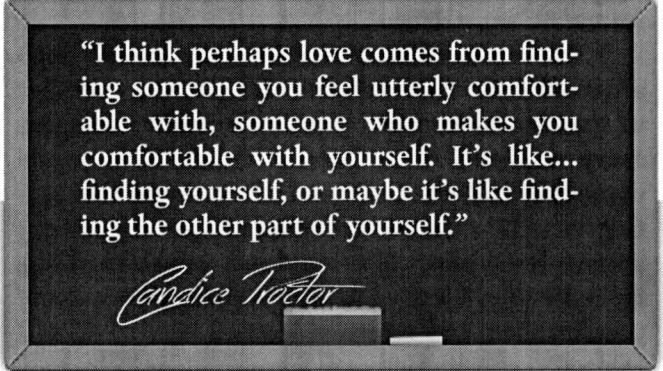

"I think perhaps love comes from finding someone you feel utterly comfortable with, someone who makes you comfortable with yourself. It's like... finding yourself, or maybe it's like finding the other part of yourself."

Candice Proctor

Moving home was not easy. Going from being an independent student to living under the same roof with my parents and abiding by their rules was a struggle. I knew I needed to move out and my goal was to make that happen as soon as possible. I found a one bedroom apartment in downtown Lancaster, bought some cheap furniture, and moved in a few months after graduation. It was not located in the best part of town, but it was mine and I had regained my independence. I felt secure until one night I was awakened by a hard knock on my back door. Standing in front of me was the owner of a small grocery store which was located caddy corner to my apartment. He stated that he had just chased an intruder off my porch and wanted to make sure I was okay. My past fears that I had buried were suddenly visible and I had nowhere to run. I told my parents about the incident at my apartment and we decided it was best to have my dog, Shoney, an Irish Setter and Labrador mix, live with me for a few days. Having her with me eased my pounding heart at night, but the reality of my past was becoming too much to bear by myself. I knew I needed to tell my secret to someone in order for me to begin to heal.

I had recently reconnected with an old high school friend, Mike Schober, who was a member of the "Famn Damily", a group of kids who spent every weekend at my parents' house. He would come over to drink, party, and talk to my parents as if they were his own. He respected my parents and my parents loved him. The bond that was formed was indescribable. I looked to him, and the others, as my own brothers and sisters. I learned how to drive, I learned the importance of friendship, and I learned to accept others because of the "Famn Damily". We were inseparable. But Mike stood out from the others. He was adorable with blonde curly hair and a smile that made me melt. He drove a yellow VW bug which I found sexy for some reason, but he was more of a friend to my family than to me. During college we would write letters back and forth and, upon my return home, we decided to go out on a date. Our first date was to the Ephrata Fair and I won a gold fish, which was our first pet, and the rest of the summer we became closer. We went to the movies, spent nights talking alone on the road to nowhere, and spent as much time together as we could before he left for his final year at Villanova. He treated me like a princess and I was falling in love, yet, I was hiding my secret. In order for our relationship to progress, I knew I needed to tell him what happened.

After just a couple of months of dating, I confessed my secret to the first person I would ever tell, the person I trusted to not look at me differently. We were sitting in the family room of my parent's home; it was just the two of us, he was holding my hand as I began to recount that night in Erie. I remember saying the words, "I was raped", and looking directly into his eyes trying to find some sign of disgust.

Instead, he wrapped me in the most gentle, warm embrace and proceeded to tell me that everything would be okay. I felt relief. My secret was no longer just mine; I now had someone I could share my thoughts, feelings, and fears with. I had someone in my life that knew about my past and still accepted me for who I was. I felt free…I felt accepted… I felt respected… I felt loved.

We married in September of 1985, one day after hurricane Gloria stormed through the northeast. After our honeymoon in the Poconos, we came home to begin our life together. In 1987, we were graced with a beautiful baby girl, Michelle Anne, a precious miracle that changed our lives. Becoming first time parents offered its own challenges and we faced each new obstacle together. From changing diapers, to chicken pox and double ear infections, we learned to tackle the unknown, have faith in each other, and trust our instincts. Two years later, we welcomed our second beautiful daughter, JoAnne Marie, and our family was happy, healthy, and thriving. Watching my girls grow was nothing short of miraculous. And then I received the news that would change my life forever. My mother had cancer.

My mom was my best friend and my girls idolized

her. From her love of Notre Dame Football to her unending love for God and others, my mother was all I strived to be. She loved to have fun and every moment of every day was filled with laughter and mischievousness. She loved to find trouble and dragged me along. She would toilet paper houses and, instead of throwing rice at a wedding, she made miniature pancakes and threw them at the bride and groom instead. She taught me to say "rabbit rabbit" on the first day of each month so that I would have good luck the entire month long. I would drive with her to the barren corn fields on News Year Eve to wish the cows "Happy New Year" because if we didn't tell them, how would they know? We would go to the mall and "people watch" and she loved to look at good-looking guys' butts as they walked past her gazing eyes. Her smile was contagious and her love for life was indescribable. When I found out that she had leiomyosarcoma, a rare form of soft tissue cancer, I didn't know what I was going to do. I couldn't bear to lose my best friend. Instead of giving up, she fought back tears and pledged that she would not give up...she had too much left to do. She underwent multiple chemotherapy treatments and radiation treatments and went back to the oncologist to have him tell her that she had only a few months to live.

"Bull shit," she exclaimed! "There is only one person in this world who knows when I am going to die and that is God. Until then, I will continue to fight!"

With that, she turned, walked away and immediately began researching experimental treatments. She knew that she did not have too much time left, but if she could help future cancer patients by trying something new, she would. That was my mom...

completely selfless and always giving. She quickly began treatments at the Fox Chase Cancer center. At this time, Michelle was in Kindergarten, so JoAnne and I would take her to treatments. I remember JoAnne sitting on my mom's lap, playing with her "gobble" (the skin that hangs under the chin) as each drip of medicine slowly filled her body with the poison that would hopefully cure her. Instead, it robbed her of her hair and her strength, but she never lost her faith. She was slowly dying before my eyes and my world would never be the same, but I knew I needed to remain strong for her and my children.

It was in late August/early September of 1993 that I began to feel tired and sick on a daily basis. I thought I was just overcome with fatigue and mental exhaustion from taking care of my mom and the passing of my grandfather, that I simply disregarded my symptoms. I decided to go to the doctor where I surprisingly discovered I was pregnant. Amidst the ugliness of cancer, a miracle was being formed.

My pregnancy was uneventful but my mom was getting worse as each day passed. On May 12, 1994, as I was in labor, my mom was receiving her last chemo treatment. She called me from her appointment to let me know that she would be by my side before I gave birth. We were in a race. I was ready to give birth and she wanted to be there to witness one last miracle of life. Instead, Stephen Michael, our third child, entered the world with my husband by my side and my mother in another hospital, connected to a machine that could no longer sustain her life. She arrived a few hours later, wrapped Stephen in her arms, and looked at me with tears in her eyes and said, "I told you I would be here!"

Four months later, on September 8, 1994, my

mother took her last breath. Death can be scary, ugly and nightmarish, but the passing of my mother was peaceful. She had been home, under the care of Hospice for a few weeks, and was lying in a coma-like state in her bed when I walked in that morning. Her breathing had become more labored and her blood pressure was slowly declining, but she was still holding on. My father left to go to the store to pick up an alarm clock, the hospice nurses were in the living room, and I was alone with my mom. I held her hand, kissed her cheek, and realized that my moments left with my best friend were soon to be over. Every single day I told my mom I loved her. Every single day I told my mom that I admired her. Every single day I told my mom how much of an inspiration she was to me and everyone who knew her. Yet, I never told her what I wish I could have told her years ago. I never told her I was raped. I leaned over, looked into her lifeless eyes, and whispered, "I was raped, Mom. I am sorry I never told you, but I didn't want you to worry about me. I know you thought I could you tell you everything, but I kept this a secret because I didn't want to see you hurt. I didn't want to see the pain that I knew this would cause you. Please forgive me." I grabbed her hand, kissed her cheek, and took a deep breath. I finally told her.

Her breathing became shallower and her pulse was barely palpable, but she continued to hold on to life. My father came back from running errands and my brother arrived soon after. We stood next to my mother's side, all three of us holding hands and quietly saying, "It's okay, mom. You can let go. We love you." As we did this, my brother looked out the sliding glass door in the bedroom and noticed a dove sitting patiently on a bird bath, staring at us with peaceful eyes. As we turned to look at the dove, my mother took her last breath and the dove flew away, carrying my mother's soul on the journey toward heaven.

It was time for me to walk in my mother's footsteps. It was time to carry on her legacy and make her proud.

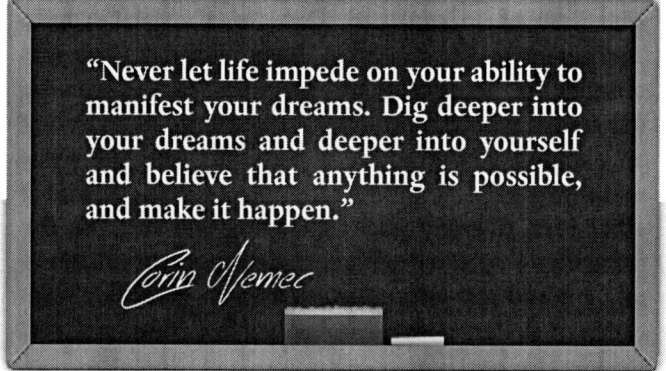

How did I go from assisting with autopsies, becoming a mom, to finally becoming a teacher? The answer was simple... I became Mrs. Pennsylvania! Where did this come from? It was a difficult process, but it was my own children that drove me to "go for the crown" without them even knowing.

One constant in raising my children was telling them to always chase their dreams and to never let anyone or anything stand in their way. Yet, I was not leading by example. When I was a little girl, I watched every Miss America and Miss USA pageant with eagerness and excitement. I was envious of their poise and beauty. And, like many other little girls, it was a dream to one day wear a crown with the sole purpose of knowing that others felt me beautiful enough to earn the title and represent the whole world (okay... it's a little girls dream!). And so, with no idea what I was getting into, in 1996, I decided to enter the Mrs. Pennsylvania International Pageant, two years after my mother died. I was doing this for my kids, true, but deep inside I was hoping to gain confidence in the search for my own identity as more than a wife and mother.

The whole process was foreign to me. I first became Mrs. Lancaster County by simply meeting the criteria and paying an entrance fee. Easy. The next step was competing. To say this was the worst part of earning the crown would be an understatement. I had to buy an evening gown, create a platform, and the most dreaded part of all, obtain and wear aerobic attire for all to see. Evening gown shopping was fun, but the price tags associated with each dress were monumental. I could not fathom purchasing a gown for hundreds of dollars to wear for only a few moments, so I decided to rent, which was a good decision. I walked away with a purple, long sleeve sequined gown that complimented me in every way possible. I felt comfortable. I actually felt pretty. Aerobic wear, however, was nothing short of hysterical. Gray leggings, black "leotard", white ankle socks with white sneakers... the thought of it makes me laugh still today. Yet, it covered me and that made me feel more confident.

With all the clothing items purchased and/or rented, I headed off to Harrisburg to begin the two-day long process of vying for the title of Mrs. Pennsylvania. The first day consisted of informational meetings and the chance to get to know the other contestants. I could lie here and say that there were 20 other women competing, but, besides myself, there were only three others! They were each beautiful, warm, and outgoing and I began to second guess myself, even though I knew the worst I could do was third runner up. The first evening ended with a cocktail party and more socializing. My nerves got the best of me and going to sleep was a battle.

The dreaded one-on-one interview competition was first thing Saturday morning, and I knew if I had a chance at all, this was it. The questions were expected: "Tell me about your family." "Discuss your platform." "Why did you decide to compete for Mrs. Pennsylvania?" After a grueling 30 minutes, the interviews were complete and it was time to prepare for the pageant. Trying to learn to "pageant walk" was not fun. I am flat-footed and my knees buckle inward making me waddle like a duck... not the picture perfect pageant legs by any means. I laughed my way through the practice and learned everything I could in a short few hours of time. I was going to go through with this and prove to my kids, and myself, that you should never give up on your dreams.

The pageant began and I was a bundle of nerves. From the introduction, to modeling aerobic wear and evening gown and the dreaded on stage interview question, I struggled through with a smile on my face and a growing confidence. I was doing what I thought I would never be able to accomplish - I was doing my best and having fun while competing for a beauty queen title. I felt at peace. I felt relaxed.

The time came for the announcement.... It was down to two: a beautiful woman that I was certain was going to win and me. We held hands tightly, and stared into each other's eyes as the announcer said: "And, the new Mrs. Pennsylvania International for 1996 is... Anne Schober"! I remember looking at the audience and seeing my girls cheering, my father proudly smiling, and my sister and brother ringing cow bells! As my husband placed the crown on my head, the song "Wind Beneath my Wings" began playing. It was my special song I shared with my mom. I cried, hugged my husband tightly, and realized that my mother was with me. She would always be with me.

The next few weeks were whirlwinds of time and events. I participated in parades, newspaper and radio interviews, and prepared for the National Pageant which was being held in Tyler, Texas. My state director decided I should purchase a gown, which I did, and my aerobic attire was given to me by the National office… a one piece, grape purple, spandex leotard! Try and picture that! When I arrived in Texas, I was greeted by 50 beautiful, strong, confident pageant titleholders. I looked at my husband and quickly said, "Get me out of here. I don't belong here!" He quietly nudged me in the door and I was left on my own. I met my roommate, Mrs. Nevada, and she seemed sweet and natural. This was not her first pageant, like me, but she was not a professional either. She came to Texas with an interview book filled with possible questions we could be asked and an iron so she could flatten her money so that it would not take up extra room in her wallet. She was unique, caring, and quirky. We became quick friends and I began to enjoy the experience. The appearances at Louisiana Downs race track, shopping malls, and other destinations were meant to make us feel like movie stars, and I did. I loved signing autographs and the attention we were given was royal. But, the fun soon came to an end when the preparations for the actual pageant began. Learning that we had to do an opening dance number was the worst news I could have received. If you have ever seen Elaine dance on Seinfeld, that is me. My legs do not move to the beat, they move to their own music. Unless I have had a few beers, I do not dance and, since drinking at the pageant was unacceptable, I knew I was doomed. Learning the Macarena was fun, but the Line dances were a challenge. The producers studied us as we danced and moved the better dancers up front and placed the others in various positions. I was placed in the **very, very, very** back and that was just fine by me! I felt like I could hide from the television cameras. I felt safe.

The day of the National competition began with one-on-one interviews which counted for 50% of the overall total score. I felt relaxed as I walked into the room and saw seven stone-faced judges staring at me. I offered them my best smile, stepped to the first judge, held out my hand and said, "Good morning. My name is Anne Schober, Mrs. Pennsylvania International, and it is a pleasure to meet you." The interviews began, allowing me five minutes with each judge. I remember two questions that were asked and my answers were unique, creative, fun and me! "If you could have any dream come true, what would it be?" I smiled, took a deep breath and went for it... "My first dream is that my family will always be healthy and happy and, without sounding too selfish, I would have to say that I wish to die in a vat of chocolate with a cigarette in one hand and a beer in the other". Needless to say, that was the only question the judge asked me. He laughed the rest of the four minutes of the interview. Another judge asked how they would be able to remember me when I walked out on the stage. This was a little more difficult, but I immediately thought of my aerobic outfit and answered: "You will see two, one-piece purple aerobic outfits on stage this evening. One will be worn by a woman who is pregnant. I will be the other one… the long, purple grape instead of the round one! Almost like a withered raisin." It was the perfect answer coming from me. The interviews continued on and I felt more comfortable with each question asked of me.

The night of the competition came and I was a bundle of nerves. Would I remember the dance moves? Would I mess up my name when it came time for introductions? Would I trip and fall in the evening gown? These thoughts were like freight trains racing through my brain as the evening drew closer.

I slipped into my introductory outfit and headed on stage for the introductions and opening number, waving proudly as my time came to step up to the microphone to announce my name and state title. The music began for the opening number and there I was, in the last row, dancing my heart out. I remembered the dance moves and was bopping along when suddenly *it* happened. The music stopped. I had no idea what happened. I had no idea what do. I looked to my left and said to Mrs. North Dakota, "Shit! What the hell do we do now?" We both just started laughing but continued dancing, messing up move after move. Not having dancing abilities is hard enough with music; imagine trying to dance without music! The cameras were still rolling and little did I know that they had focused their attention on ME! Mrs. Pennsylvania caught swearing on National television. Oh my!

The pageant concluded and while I didn't place (but, I did place second in the interview losing only to the overall winner!), I was proud of myself for having lived out my dream of being a "beauty queen", if only for a brief amount of time.

When I arrived home, I immediately began visiting schools and spreading the message of the importance of raising self-esteem in children, which was my platform during the pageant. It was a tumultuous time of meeting wonderful, smiling, and energetic children, parents, teachers and school administrators along the way. Whether I was riding in a parade, chasing a greased pig at a town fair, or reading a story to a group of elementary children, I was constantly asked if I was a teacher. I was told how well I interacted with kids and that I should consider becoming a teacher as a profession. And that was when the seed of becoming a teacher was planted. As my days of Mrs. Pennsylvania came to an end, my life as a teacher was just beginning.

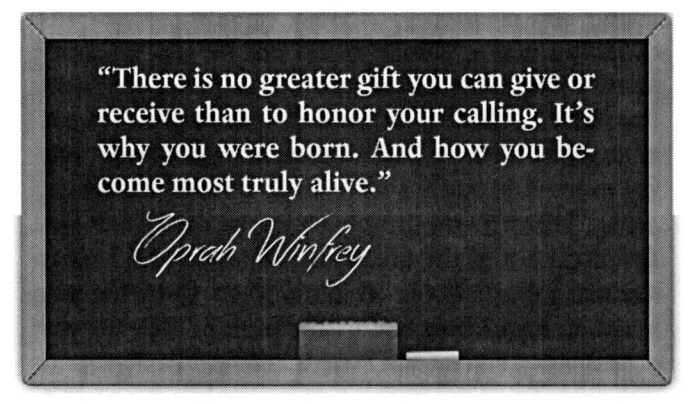

> "There is no greater gift you can give or receive than to honor your calling. It's why you were born. And how you become most truly alive."
>
> *Oprah Winfrey*

Applying to college, for the second time, was easy. Getting accepted, however, was a little more difficult. My college transcripts were not anything of which I could be proud. I passed my Medical Assistant classes at Gannon University, but my general education classes were another story. In order to have to have credits transfer, you must get at least a "C" in the class. I had a few that would qualify, but not many. My meeting with the admissions officer was intimidating. She was nonplussed and did not have a "warm fuzzy" personality as she greeted me with a generic head nod. As she looked over my transcripts, her demeanor became a little more subdued. After what seemed like an eternity, she looked at me and said I was accepted, with twelve credits being transferable, plus I was to be placed on academic probation for one year. I didn't know if I should laugh, cry or scream. Instead, I stood, shook her hand, thanked her, and immediately registered myself for the first eighteen credits I would need to become an English teacher.

I never thought I would be a teacher; being a fulltime mom was the most fulfilling job I had ever had. Seeing my children grow into beautiful, smart and outgoing young people could not be topped, but I knew I was being called into this selfless profession. But, why English? That answer was simple. I cheated my way through history class in high school, writing every date and trivial fact on my legs and up my arms. History was simply boring to me. Math was definitely out of the question. I have no idea how to balance a check book, let alone know the difference between logarithms and quadrilaterals. Science was a possibility, since I did have a medical background, but chemistry and physics were never my strong suit. English seemed a natural choice, and really the only option I had left. Reading and writing were my hobbies, so what better way to take my natural talents and expand upon them? I was going to be an English teacher!

Going back to school was difficult and life-changing. Raising three kids, trying to be a good wife, babysitting the neighbor's children while doing school work proved to be challenging. I would study when the kids were asleep, spend all day on campus while the kids were in school, and study and write until the wee hours of the morning. I was one of the oldest students in each of my classes and felt out of place many times over. When I received my first failing grade on a paper written for my Literary Criticism class, I cried and felt defeated. What was I doing? I was 35 years old and questioned myself constantly. But, I knew that in order to achieve my dream of being a teacher, I would have many hiccups along the way. I sought help from my professors, focused on my goal, and graduated in December of 2001 with a BS degree in English Education. My GPA was a solid 3.87! I was ready to begin my career.

Part Two
Untold Stories

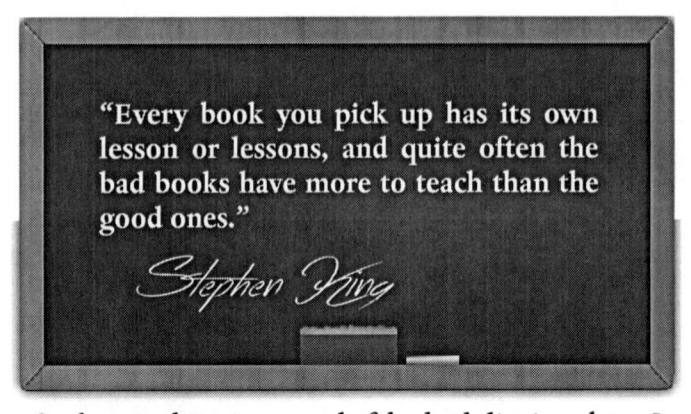

> "Every book you pick up has its own lesson or lessons, and quite often the bad books have more to teach than the good ones."
>
> *Stephen King*

Student teaching in a wonderful school district where I felt comfortable and accepted was the best place I could have learned how to be a teacher. My cooperating teacher loved writing and implemented Writers Workshops in each of her classes. Each day provided new insights and new lessons which helped to form my foundation of becoming an English teacher. I was offered a long term substitute position in the same building after my graduation, and my dream of being a teacher was quickly becoming a reality. I loved working with eighth graders and the school district, but I knew that my position was not going to be available for the following year, which was heartbreaking. I sent resumes to every school district in Lancaster County and landed a job teaching Senior English at Columbia Sr/Jr High School, a suburban, blue collar school district located close to my home.

The year started off with energy and big dreams. I filled my classroom with inspirational posters, vibrant colors and hope. Each of my classes were unique and held an eclectic group of students of who immediately stole my heart; the faces I met each day are still engraved in my heart. From the intensity shown on basketball or football game days to the quiet nervousness of uncertainty, each student was special to me.

Columbia school district was classified as low income and transient. Almost on a daily basis, a new student would enter and another would leave. It was hard to form relationships when you did not know if they were coming back the next day. It was challenging trying to teach to "the test" when they were not invested in their academics. It was a tough school district, but I loved the smallness and warmth I felt from the students and the faculty. I was trying my best to reach the kids and make literature relevant to their lives, to make them care about what they were learning. I was a new teacher and every lesson I planned was foreign to me. I tried to be creative and to form connections. Sometimes I succeeded, but, on many occasions I failed.

I remember a group of students who were struggling with understanding Arthur Miller's play *The Crucible*. I knew I had to do something different in order to help them make a connection so I planned a "trick". I began the class by being late, on purpose. I immediately walked to my desk pretending to look for a $20 bill that was left out in the open. With all eyes on me, I began my act. I promptly began to question the class and asked if anyone saw someone take the money that had been on my desk. The room became silent. I asked again. Silence. I pretended to become more agitated telling the class that the money taken was to be used for a class treat for THEM. Silence. I took my acting to a new level and began getting really, really angry. I started screaming and telling them how much I respected them and trusted them and now that was taken away. My face became red and my heart was racing. I then yelled, "Somebody took MY money and YOU need to figure out who it was!" With those words, I stomped out of the room, slammed the door, and waited quietly outside to listen to what they were saying. One young lady, Jussenya, a beautiful soul with a passion that was beyond words, stood up, came to the front of the room and began to take control. She asked each person who took the money, and, receiving no help, she promptly pulled money from her pocket and placed it on my desk. She asked the others to follow.

As she was taking over my class, I was standing in the hallway, tears streaming down my humbled cheeks. This was not part of the plan. I wanted them to get angry at me for accusing them of something that they were not! Instead, they wanted to help me! I walked back into the room and began to tell them of my plan. At first they were angry with me, which they deserved to be! That was the purpose. Just as the girls in *The Crucible* falsely accused others of witchery, I had accused them of being thieves. And then, because of one beautiful young lady and her compassion and love for me, she brought the class together and ruined my perfect lesson. While my English lesson may have failed, the life lesson was more important.

However, I failed them on so many levels. I did not get to learn their stories, who they were, and what they were all about. I failed to take the time to KNOW them. I failed to make the personal connections that could have made a difference in the classroom. For that, I will never be able to forgive myself. But, I didn't know how. I did not receive the guidance from the administration that I so desperately sought. I did not have the tools available to teach at-risk kids. I was lost, and so were they.

I remember one young man who sat in my classroom and kept falling out of his chair. I didn't know what to do and I could not keep control of the kids because of the constant attention being drafted in his direction. He would fall, get up, climb back into his desk chair, and proceed to fall again. The laughter which ensued was insurmountable. I decided to call the office and was promptly told to call the nurse. After a few moments, the nurse came to my door, took the young man downstairs for an eye test, which he passed, and he returned to my room, falling promptly asleep. I ignored him for the rest of the class period. I was lost. What do I do with a student who is visibly "under the influence" and yet returns to the classroom with no consequences? I should have talked to him…

I remember another young man who held a special place in my heart. He was a respectful and courteous student who always took the time to say good morning. While he sometimes sauntered late into class, he did so with a smile on his face and an apology on his lips. Not a day would go by that the two of us would not laugh about something. I loved his honesty, openness, and vitality. That is why I was shocked when one day something unforeseen came crashing down. It was a typical day in class and I was passing papers back to each of the students, calling them up one by one. When I got to his paper, he walked up to me, grabbed the paper, and whispered right behind my ear, "I am going to put a fucking hole in your head". I turned around, searched his eyes, and saw nothing but vacancy. I asked, "Excuse me? What did you just say?" He simply sneered and walked back to his desk. I was shaking the rest of the day and decided to speak with the principal. During our meeting, it was decided that "if" he really said those things to me, then I should report him to the police. I knew that if I did that, this young man's future would be forever in jeopardy. I kept silent. I received no backing, support or comfort from the administration. The realization that the principal did not believe me was infuriating. Again, I felt lost. This young man continued to remain a student in my classroom, but a distance between us was now evident. I failed to learn his story....

I remember a beautiful young lady who had an edge to her but I felt we had a good understanding of each other. All that changed one day when she walked into class and promptly called me a "fucking bitch". I was dumbfounded. Never before had I heard her utter those words to anyone. I decided to quietly ignore her outburst thinking it had to be once and done. However, she did not stop there. She continued calling me that same name ten times over. I stood in the classroom and cried. She had won. She had broken me down. I called the office, the principal came up to remove her from the classroom, and I knew that she would be back. Ten days later, she was back in my classroom and that is when I gave notice to the administration that I was going to leave. I had decided I wasn't going to learn her story...

That, to this day, still upsets me. What if I had taken the time to *know* her? What if I had taken the time to talk with her? To learn who she was? If I did, would the outcome have been different? Would my teacher journey have changed? Making the decision to leave was a mix of numerous emotions but one that I knew must be made.

Saying goodbye to this group of students was one of the hardest things I have ever done. How was I going to tell them that I was leaving them? I knew some would feel betrayed, but I also knew the majority would not care. Slowly my classes came in for the day and the news spread like gossip through the halls. I had students standing at my door, asking me if what they heard was true. I found one young lady in the bathroom, curled up in the corner, crying. A wonderful young man, David Smith, was visibly upset and asked to meet with me. I knew it was going to be hard saying goodbye to him. He is one who still holds a close connection with my heart. I remember the struggles he was encountering while trying to figure out who he was. Was he a jock? An actor? A singer? Could he be all of these combined? His mind was confused and he looked to me for advice. I was touched by his trust, confidence, and security he felt by seeking my thoughts. He was the first student I can remember who trusted me. And leaving him, and the others, was not going to be easy. Would they ever understand? Would they blame themselves? Would they forgive me?

My heart was melting, and yet I knew that leaving this school was the best thing for me. I had to take a stand for myself because the administration had let me down. However, the raw emotions of that day never left my heart. The last day was emotional; crying with each student, hugging them one last time, and leaving the classroom for the final time. Leaving Columbia was one of the hardest things I ever had to do. Leaving behind the building and administration was easy; leaving my students behind was hard. I left that day with a downtrodden step that echoed as my tears fell silently to the ground. I knew I had failed them. I held back unsure of myself as a teacher, unaware of the power of connections, and forever those

feelings will never go away.
I failed to make connections....

✻ ✻ ✻

I was a junior in high school, who was a confused jock. I played on the football team, but also played a major part in our high school's drama department, and even more confusing, a starting member of our quiz bowl team. I had not begun to find my identity in this world, and like most typical sixteen year olds, I felt that the world had been stacked against me. Fortunately for me our school had just hired a new eleventh grade English teacher in the form of Mrs. Anne Schober.

Leading up to this point in my life, I had spent my life feeling like I was a second-class teenager; failing to win the big games, never able to land a principle role in our school's productions, sitting on the bench behind players I felt weren't as talented as me. I was slightly overweight, and I felt as though the world would never give me a break. Enter Mrs. Schober, the woman who gave me the courage to be who I am, and never stop fighting for what I believe in.

I was never much of a writer. I loved to write, I would jot down storylines I had in my head, but was never able to bring any of these ideas to fruition. Then came the assignment that changed everything. Write a personal essay for the Scholastic Writing Competition. I knew exactly what I would write about: my life's failures. I mean, as a teen, failures have this way of looming over you like a rain cloud in a comic strip. I had plenty of material to draw from, and a teacher, who regardless of the self-loathing content, encouraged and helped me write my "masterpiece".

I began writing, and I wrote with vigor. Finally, I had a chance to tell the world how I had been wronged my entire life. Seriously, the world needed to know that my little league baseball team, The Cubs, made it to the World Series four consecutive years, only to lose each and every time (not to mention, they won the first year after I had aged out of that specific league). It was also vital for the world to hear how I rode the bench on my basketball team in Jr. High, and also in Varsity Football. I poured my heart into this personal essay, and never once did Mrs. Schober tell me I should change my topic, or that my writing was poor (which coincidentally it was, grammatical errors all over the place). She believed in me. For the first time, I felt that someone believed in me, wanted to hear what I had to say, and honestly wanted to see me succeed.

I finished my personal essay with a concluding paragraph that would bring any grown man (who was overweight, or overlooked during childhood) to tears. I slapped the title, Second Best: The Story of My Life, on top, and sent it off to Scholastic to be judged. I didn't feel confident about my chances, and honestly expected to hear nothing of it. Lo and behold it won a Gold Key, and was entered into the national competition. This was a changing point in my life.

Knowing that someone supports you can change a person's life. And it did.

I suddenly had confidence. I earned a leading role in our school's production of Les Miserables the following year, was a starter on my football team. The confidence that Mrs. Schober instilled in me while helping me find my voice shaped who I am today. She did nothing but encourage me to follow my dreams.

And then Mrs. Schober did the worst thing she could have possibly done.

She left.

Halfway through my senior year, she was offered her dream position at her alma mater. I was crushed. If she taught me anything, it was to write. So I wrote her a letter. Telling her how much she had changed my life, how I wish she wasn't leaving, but also that I understood. She read this letter before the day was over, and when I went to see her during my lunch period; her classroom was full of other grieving students. She spoke with them for a bit, but eventually kicked everyone out, and grieved with me personally.

I have never felt a wider range of emotions than I did in that moment. I was devastated to see her leave, but she just made time to grieve with me personally and made me feel like I was the most important person in her world during this incredibly difficult transition for her. If that doesn't grow your self-esteem than I'm not sure what will.

Today I am not a professional writer, but her love and unwavering support has never left me. I now live in Chicago, where I am a struggling actor. I am following my dreams, and I have her to thank for that. Beyond the lessons, and the textbooks, and the tests is where Mrs. Schober teaches from, and her students learn more than they could ever hope.

David Smith, Student

> "You must recognize, embrace, and be honest about what is real for you today and allow that understanding to inform the choices you make. Only then will you be able to build the future of your dreams."
>
> *Suze Orman*

I needed a sign... Walking into Lancaster Catholic for the first time as a teacher was surreal. So many memories came flooding back to me of when I was a student within these same four walls. Nothing had changed. The smell was still powerfully old, some of my teachers still graced their same classrooms, and the same graffiti-filled desks were still stoically in place. This was my new home and one where I knew I belonged, but I still had doubts. Did I make the right choice? I turned to God and pleaded for him to send me a sign that I was in the place where I was needed most, and this sign came to me in a powerful instant. My first day.

I had taken my middle daughter, JoAnne, to school early for an early morning soccer practice which began promptly at six AM. I knew this would be a perfect time for me to get to my classroom early, get the feel of the room, and just breathe. The building was eerily quiet. I was lost in my thoughts when suddenly my daughter appeared at my door, crying and shaking. She had just been told that a beloved teacher was killed the night before in a tragic accident. A group of teachers were on their way home from attending a funeral when an eighteen wheeler crashed into the back of the car, killing the teacher instantly. As I tried to grasp with the reality of the horrendous event, I knew God needed me here, in this place, to help my own children and the many others I had yet to meet on a day that would forever change our lives.

I immediately called Michelle, my oldest daughter, and told her the news. She was crying and asking so many questions of which I had no answers. Her best friend's mother had died. All I wanted to do was crawl through the telephone lines and hug her and wish for all of this to go away. As the students began to enter the building, you could feel the sadness. You could feel the quiet. You could feel the heartache. When I saw Michelle, we hugged each other tightly and cried. It was a surreal moment for both of us as we tried to come to grips with the reality of loss. Minutes passed and the entire school gathered in the gymnasium to be told of the accident, to be together as a family, and to grieve, cry and pray. How was I going to teach when a beloved faculty member had just died? What was I going to say to a collective group of students that had no idea who I was? This was not my idea of a first day, but I knew what I had to do. I listened. I prayed with my students. I helped them grapple with questions, fears and realities. I did not know any of my student's names on that first day, but it didn't matter. I knew I was in the place where I was meant to be. I was home.

It was time to make connections...

Part Three
Stories Spoken

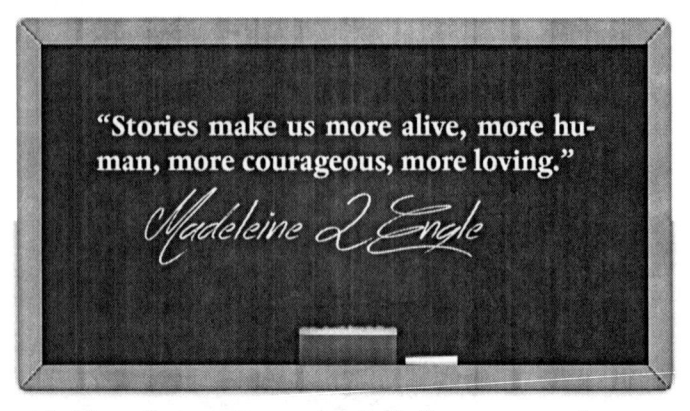

> "Stories make us more alive, more human, more courageous, more loving."
>
> *Madeleine L'Engle*

My first days at Lancaster Catholic, my new home, were a blur. I barely had time to breathe. I wanted so much to succeed, to teach better and learn more. I volunteered to moderate clubs; I skipped lunch to spend time with my students. I was given a new class, Academic Skills, as well as my Senior and Junior class loads, and jumped at the chance to do whatever I could for the students and the school. I became more comfortable with my role as a teacher, and I felt that I was making a difference. That all became clear during the first week of school for the 2004/2005 school year. I was discussing with my seniors their summer reading books, hoping to begin a good conversation about themes, characters and the power a book holds. I was getting nowhere. No one was volunteering to discuss what they read. It was SILENT. I had to do something, and what happened next changed my teaching in a dramatic way.

    I don't know what caused me to do so, but I began discussing a book I had read over the summer ... Some say it was divine intervention; I agree. I had never discussed my personal life in a classroom before, and what I was about to do could easily get me fired. But, I knew I was being called to do what I never imagined... I began to tell my story...

"Some say I was lucky."

I gently closed the tattered and frayed pages of the book I was reading to my class and glanced at the soundless students sitting in front of me. As I began to explain the premise of the book to my seniors, my voice shook.

"Alice Sebold, the author of *Lucky*, was raped at the age of eighteen. Her memoir was written to save her life and, in return, it saved mine."

My heart began beating louder and harder. I closed my eyes so that the tears could stay hidden. I took a deep breath and did something I never thought I would do. I began recounting my own rape to a group of seniors in my World Literature class.

"I remember that night as if it was yesterday. I was in a room. With a man. Paralyzed by booze and fear. Music blaring – the sound of Queen was drowning out my screams. It was just the two of us. I was trembling; he was in control. I was scared for my life; he was growing more powerful and determined with every "no" I scream. He was stealing my innocence; I was letting him walk away. And, because I tell no one, he raped six other young women."

I took a deep breath, opened my tear filled eyes, and placed myself back into the classroom, where I was no longer just a teacher; I was now a person, a victim, a human. The students were silent and dazed, and as I glanced around the room, my eyes were drawn toward Erin. I witnessed the once-twinkling eyes become blurry. Just moments ago she was giggly and energetic. Just moments ago she was the girl who seemed perfect. The beautiful blonde-haired girl that every boy wanted to date and every girl wished to look like was suddenly clothed in terror. Erin, the typical American girl who was accepted into her dream college, who was a member of the Homecoming Court, who had many friends and received good grades, was falling apart before my eyes.

As the class departed, Erin stayed glued in her seat. I walked over and wrapped my arms tightly around her. She began to sob. She was raped only two weeks prior and I was the first person she told. After Erin recounted what happened to her that horrible night, I grasped her by the arms and stared into her broken eyes, realizing that what I was about to tell her was something that I wished had been said to me years ago when I needed it most: "I love you." I whispered those three simple, yet powerful, words over and over as we rocked gently together, alone in an abandoned classroom, crying for something we knew we would never have again. We survived. We were lucky.

I will never know the reason I was drawn to tell my story that day, but because I did I helped a beautiful young woman realize that what happened to her was not going to define her.

But, telling my story was not a heroic deed; it came with criticism and punishment. I was called to the office to discuss what happened in my classroom and why I decided it was important to tell such a horrific and personal story. I talked; administration listened. I was reprimanded and a letter was placed in my file. I walked deflated back to my classroom and waited for my next to class to arrive, ready once again tell my story, if I was meant to do so.

We connected through a common story and wounded hearts.

*   *   *

All these years later and I still hate the woods, 40 ounce beer bottles in a brown paper bag, baseball caps worn backwards and rap music blaring with the bass pounding loudly to drown out my thoughts. It has been eight years and still it feels like yesterday; a memory that haunts me and awakens me at night.

I received a phone call from my best guy friend asking me to join him and another guy for a party. I was excited because despite my outward appearances, I was very shy and did not socialize as much as my other friends. My life was messed up; my parents had divorced just a year earlier and all the craziness was wearing on me. Being asked to a party made me feel like I was on top of the world. He asked me to meet him at the town deli, where we worked, and we would drive together to the party. I knew tonight would be fun and would help me take my mind off what was happening at home.

I saw a silver Eclipse pull up to the deli, which surprised me because that was not my friends car; instead it was his friend's car and I immediately felt a little uncomfortable. They told me to hop into the back and we were off to the party. However, on the way, my friend received a call from his father telling him he had to come home immediately. I asked if I could be dropped off first, but the driver said "No" and would instead take me to my car AFTER he drops off my friend. I was getting a bad "vibe" and thought I should get out of the car with my friend, but I was told he would take me to my car.

After dropping my friend off, the driver asked me to get in the front seat. We started heading toward the deli but instead of stopping, he kept driving. My heart began beating harder; I should have gotten out of the car with my friend. When I asked where we were going, he said, "I will show you in a minute". As the rain started falling from the sky, I grew more and more scared. He pulled onto a gravel, dirt road and parked the car in the middle of the woods. I immediately grabbed for my cell phone and quickly noticed "no service" flashing at the top of the screen. As the driver pulled out a "40", he began reminiscing about our younger school days, mocking me because he always picked on me. As he kept drinking, he began flirting and asked me to kiss him since we never did in middle school. I said no, and he kept persisting. I kept saying "No, No, No" and suddenly I felt his forearm come across my neck.

I remember trying to hit him, I remember crying. I remember thinking how stupid I was. I remember him saying "This is what people do. Doesn't it feel good?" I remember wanting to throw up as he continued to rape me. I remember thinking that my life would never be the same.

After he had his way with me, he drove me to my car. What was only a couple of miles felt like an eternity. As I quickly ran out of the car, I heard him as he was leaning out his window say, "Hey now, no need to tell anyone... our secret". I sat in my car, windows up, doors locked, and cried for 35 minutes. I drove home, shaking, scared and disgusted with myself, showered and cried myself to sleep knowing that no one will ever want me again. I was damaged goods.

I was supposed to go on a date the next day, but I silently knew he wouldn't want me, so I cancelled. I spent the rest of my summer break not sleeping and becoming more withdrawn. I hated myself. I hated him. I hated my life.

My senior year began and I remember being excited for school; it was a welcome break from my thoughts. I remember walking into my senior English course and being happy about being in this class. Mrs. Schober started talking about summer reading and the different books she read. She then began to talk about Lucky, a memoir written by Alice Sebold, which recounts the author's rape while she was in college. While talking about the book, I noticed my teacher become teary eyed as she began to tell the class the story of her own rape. I remember hearing her voice quiver as she began… "I was at a party…in college…started drinking …he told me I was beautiful…." I couldn't believe what I was hearing. I remember thinking that I was meant to hear this today, I was meant to be in this class.

The bell rang and the class left; I didn't want to leave. I knew that if I didn't say something now, I never would. While I don't remember the exact words we exchanged that day, I do remember holding each other, crying, and knowing that she understood. But, more than anything else, I knew I could trust her and I knew that she would help me. We talked a lot during my senior year; sometimes my friends would join us. I felt safe in Room 123.

Rape hurts more than anyone can imagine. It makes you feel alone; it makes you feel like an outsider. I still feel like people can see my secret and I still feel scared. I still don't like who I am; my self-esteem and confidence was shattered within seconds. Being raped took everything away from me, but Mrs. Schober helped me to see I was no longer alone. We are lucky to have each other.

Erin Gannon, Student

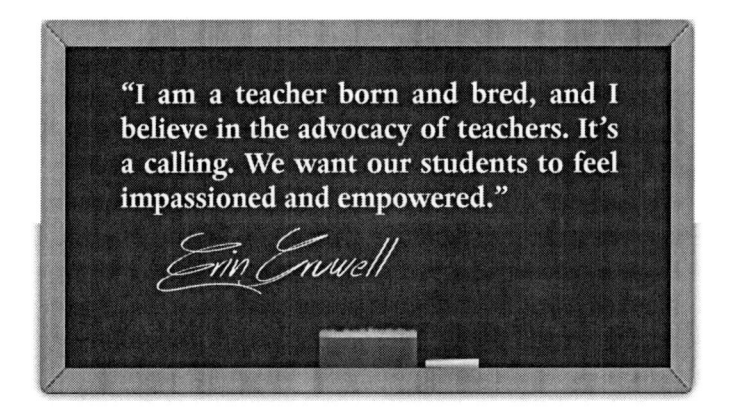

> "I am a teacher born and bred, and I believe in the advocacy of teachers. It's a calling. We want our students to feel impassioned and empowered."
>
> *Erin Gruwell*

"Oh my gosh" are the three words I uttered over and over and over again as I listened to the woman on the other end of the phone inviting me to become a Freedom Writer teacher. It was June, 2007, and I was on the phone talking to Erin Gruwell, the Freedom Writer teacher who inspired the movie, *The Freedom Writers,* starring Hillary Swank and Patrick Dempsey. Erin Gruwell was inviting me to Long Beach to train with her and her students! How did this happen?

My daughter, Michelle, came home one evening and began discussing a movie she had watched the night before and told me that it reminded her of me. I became intrigued and decided to watch *Freedom Writers* for myself. What I viewed was inspirational, moving, and life-changing. A young teacher went into a public high school in Long Beach, California, and cared about the students that no one else wanted to teach. Because of her compassion, empathy, and courage, she guided all 150 of her students to graduate from high school, and eventually, college. I wanted to know more and immediately began looking for more information online. I came across the Freedom Writers Foundation website which mentioned that educators could apply to become Freedom Writer teachers. I knew I needed to submit my application. Upon reading the qualifications, I immediately realized that my dream was not to be. In one of the very first paragraphs of the application instructions it stated teachers who work in the public sector, detention centers and other facilities, may apply. My heart sank. I was a teacher in a private, parochial school. I knew I had to learn from this amazing teacher, so I did not let the word "public" get in my way. I immediately sat down at the computer and answered each question thoughtfully and with my heart, just as Erin did when she taught. I decided to base my essay on the fact that it did not matter if a child was in a private school, a Catholic school, in a detention center or in a public school – a kid is a kid. Once you realize that, then you have gained much. I sent off my application and held my breath. Months passed and I heard nothing. And then, on June 13, 2007, I received the phone call that would change my life as a teacher and a person. I was chosen from among 10,000 applicants to join the Freedom Writers world! I was about to become one of 150 teachers nationwide to work, learn, and train with this amazing teacher.

On July 20, 2007, I boarded a plane headed to Los Angeles, California! After a six-hour plane ride, I stepped off the plane, was greeted by an enthusiastic Freedom Writer teacher and immediately met a few others that were joining me on this incredible journey. We boarded a van which transported us to a five star hotel where we were each given a private room with king sized beds. Luxury abounded everywhere I looked! What did I do to deserve such grandiose accommodations? After relaxing and meeting the twenty other chosen teachers for this institute, we boarded the vans for our first chance to meet Erin Gruwell and some of her Freedom Writer students.

We drove past Wilson High School, where Erin taught, and it all started to seem "real" to me. I was no longer living a dream; I was beginning a journey of a lifetime. As we arrived at the Freedom Writer Foundation headquarters, I was in awe. Erin Gruwell was standing at the door, ready to greet each of us by name. As I approached her, my heart was pumping voraciously. We hugged tightly and I cried. (Yes, I am a "bubbler", as my dad calls me!). I could not believe that I was standing in the same room as a woman who had inspired so many. And now I was to become one of her students and learn from the best.

The next five days were filled with a whirlwind of activity. From People Bingo, the Line Game, Toast for Change, a private screening of the *Freedom Writers* movie at Paramount Studios, salsa dancing, Coat of Arms, Museum of Tolerance, meeting Holocaust survivor Renee Silverstone, writing, crying, and celebrating, my life as a teacher became powerfully transformed. I knew that when I walked back into my classroom for the first time as a Freedom Writer teacher, nothing would ever be the same. I would never miss another story. I would teach my students empathy, acceptance, and tolerance. I would teach them that each person has a story and each person deserves to be heard.

But how was I going to do this? One of the first lessons Erin taught was to enlighten us on her "secret" of reaching even the most unreachable student. She came up with her own ingredients for success and shared this valuable recipe with us, her novice group of teachers, who were on the edge of their seats hanging on her every word. Erin said that if we followed the ingredients to her special sauce, we too, would find success in our own classrooms.

Ms. G's Secret Sauce
1. *Believe in your students*
2. *Break down comfort zones*
3. *Establish a safe environment*
4. *Validate prior knowledge*
5. *Motivate your students*
6. *Encourage collaboration*
7. *Teach tolerance*
8. *Promote diversity*
9. *Create community*
10. *Build bridges*
11. *Expect accountability*
12. *Celebrate success*

We placed each of these ingredients into action during our five days in Long Beach, and learned firsthand the power of creating connections and getting to know our students. It was time to take all that I learned from Erin, her students, and the other teachers I was blessed to know and work with during our time in Long Beach, and get to work!

The day I set foot into my classroom in August of 2007, I knew that I would never be the teacher I once was. I was setting out on a new path and the future seemed bright, challenging, and daunting. I was given a challenge from Erin Gruwell...I was going to change lives by engaging, enlightening and empowering **each** of my students by using the secret ingredients. I was ready to teach from my heart.

I was ready to make connections.

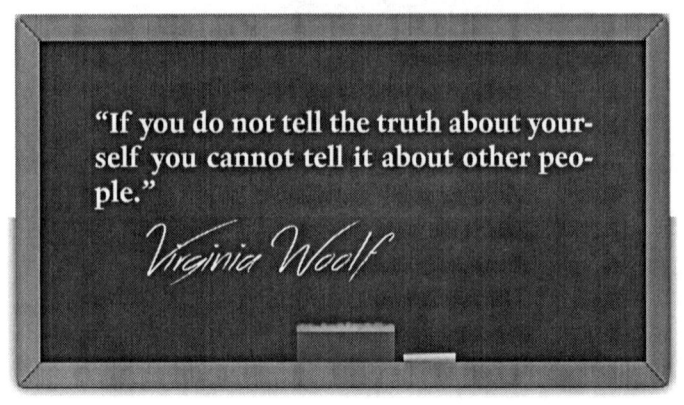

> "If you do not tell the truth about yourself you cannot tell it about other people."
>
> *Virginia Woolf*

SECRET INGREDIENT #1
Believe in your Students

At Lancaster Catholic, a new initiative was introduced where those students who scored lowest on the placement exam would be given a class where they received extra study help and the skills needed to enhance their regular studies. This was to be my third year of teaching this course, but it would never be the same. This class would be the first set of Freedom Writers from Lancaster Catholic and I would be their teacher for the next four years. In August of 2007, eighteen freshmen students walked into room 123 and quickly left their footprints on my heart.

Bonding as a class was not easy. The walls were up and they were not coming down. I had students who were told they were stupid and would never graduate. I had students who were living in poverty. I had a student who was Jewish and attending a Catholic school; he felt isolated. I had a student who was in and out of a rehab center. I had students who were fighting inner demons. I had students who just wanted to be respected but did not know where to begin. Most of the students in this class were from the city and coming to Lancaster Catholic brought about many challenges including academics, discipline, and socialization.

In order to get to know my students better, we began writing diary entries, sharing our stories with each other, and bonding as a class. It wasn't easy. There were many days when no one would share, and then other days when the tears were flowing. On several occasions, I found it necessary to read my own entries so that the students felt comfortable. As the days waned on, I could see the transformation beginning; my students were becoming a family. They created a name for themselves, "The Mix", because they were a group of kids from different schools, experiences, and ethnicities. They created a class slogan, "Mix us up and we stay tight because we are the Mix and we do what's right". I was so proud of all they were accomplishing and I knew it was because I believed in them. If one of my Mix kids got in trouble, I was there to figure out what I could do to help. If one was struggling with personal issues, I was there to listen. If a teacher belittled them, I became their cheerleader. I believed in them because they deserved nothing less. At one faculty meeting, I was voted "the one most likely to take a bullet for his/her students", and that was nothing short from the truth. They had been told they were stupid and "different" from so many others; it was my job to build them up and help them to believe in themselves.

Never was this more true than with one of my students, Patrick Brennan. "P-Turtle", as we liked to call him, was a transfer student who came to Lancaster Catholic with little self-esteem when it came to academics. He was the sweetest, most likable kid you would ever meet, but his confidence was non-existent. Through journal writing and our many talks, I quickly learned that Patrick was told he was "stupid and would never graduate" from teachers at his old school. How can you build a student up when he has been shattered and belittled by those who are supposed to help and guide? My heart broke for him. P-Turtle quickly gained entrance into my heart with his innocent smile and gigantic heart, and when I was given an opportunity for him to confront the teachers who spoke so horribly of him, I knew we had to take the chance.

After becoming a Freedom Writer teacher, I had been asked to speak to students from middle school through college about the Freedom Writers and the importance of writing. When I received a call to speak at Patrick's old school, I knew that he would have to join me. When I approached Patrick with my idea, he was scared and uncertain. He wanted to face his biggest critic, but was he really ready? He discussed the idea with his parents, and with their blessing, we marched into his old school ready to show them that Patrick Brennan would not only graduate, but he was one hell of an amazing young man!

The presentation began with an overview of the *real* Freedom Writers and the *real* Erin Gruwell. It was going great and, glancing at Patrick, I could see his nerves were beginning to overcome his strength. I showed the Prime Time video with Connie Chung, a brief news documentary about the Freedom Writers, to give me a few moments to speak with Patrick before his talk.

"Hey, P-Turtle, are you nervous?"

"Yea, I am", Patrick said, his voice cracking.

"Do you want to go through with this? Do you still want to talk? Do you still want to read in front of the entire auditorium?"

"If I don't do it now, than there may be a kid sitting in the audience who will never speak up because I didn't. I have to do this for myself, but I have to do it for the kids sitting out there who have been told they were stupid. I have to do it for us."

As the video was ending, I glanced toward the back of the auditorium and noticed that Patrick's mom had silently walked in, unnoticed. My heart melted... this was her chance to see her son face his enemies. I was overwhelmed.

After the video, it was Patrick's turn to shine. He stood up, took the microphone, and began to read an excerpt from the *Freedom Writers Diary*. You could hear his voice shake, but he kept going. Slowly and confidently, Patrick read in front of hundreds of people. He read in front of the teachers who told him he would never graduate. He read in front of the teachers who told him he was stupid.

When he finished reading, he began telling his story.

"People will put you down, but get up anyway. Believe in yourself. You will have people in your life that will tell you cannot do things and that you will not succeed, that you are too stupid or too dumb to be what you want you to be. Don't believe them. You are important. You do matter. You have a story that needs to be told, so write your life story."

It was powerful, and for the rest of the presentation, Patrick was a rock star and received a standing ovation! He was invincible and I was honored to have witnessed this transformation. I stole a glance with Patrick's mom and realized we were both crying with pride for her son and my "P-Turtle".

We connected because I believed in who they were, who they are, and who they will become...

☆ ☆ ☆

When I was asked to go back to my middle school to talk about Freedom
Writers and how the program changed my life, so many emotions went through my head. I
was mostly nervous, but a side of me was happy and proud to be returning.

When I was entering seventh and eighth grade, I was excited about the chance to experience a new school, new friends, and new opportunities. I like to use the expression "I was a small fish in a big pond". Entering the middle school I was placed in learning support style classrooms where there was only on average 10 kids per class, and we learned at a different pace than everyone else. I enjoyed being in these classrooms because I knew if I was in a normal classroom with twenty-five plus kids, I wouldn't get the help that I needed with my studies.

From the start of middle school, things were going pretty well; I was enjoying my time at school for the most part, and earning semi-decent grades. I was comfortable and ready to learn until something happened that shaped the way I acted for a while.

One day I was in school and one of my teachers told me, "You will never go far in life, and never be successful". That statement was enough to send me over the edge. From that moment on, I wanted nothing to do with school at all. I was very shook up by what she said. It stood with me every class I attended.

Ever since that teacher told me that, my parents said I had a big change in my attitude inside and outside school. I was very angry with the words I used. I did not want anything to do with school. I dreaded going to school and never did my work or studied for any tests.

Once my parents saw a huge drop in my mood, they decided to have a meeting with my teachers to discuss what was going on inside the school and why this was *happening. When the meeting ended, my parents were furious with the school and did not back down until they got the answers they wanted and I got the tools I needed to succeed, and I thank my parents to this day for fighting for my education and having my back every step of the way.*

My parents decided that staying in the school district was not the best option for me and starting looking into other schools in Lancaster county and came across Lancaster Catholic. Deciding to attend Lancaster Catholic for my high school years was the best decision my parents and myself could have made. Lancaster Catholic gave me all the confidence back as a student and made me realize that I do matter and I can achieve any dream I wanted. While at Lancaster Catholic, I met an amazing teacher to who this day I am thankful for. She pushed me to my limits and reminded me that I am someone and, if I work hard, anything is possible.

When Mrs. Schober and I walked into my old school to give a presentation to seventh grade students about the Freedom Writers, I was completely nervous. The auditorium was packed full of students and teachers and I remember thinking in my head that only a couple years ago I was sitting in those seats listening to guest speakers talk to us about the future. Today was my turn for the students to listen.

While Mrs. Schober was giving her introduction, I was looking around the auditorium and my eyes locked onto one of the teachers who told me I would amount to nothing and not be successful. I wanted to run, but the other part of me stayed because I wanted her to know that what she told me wasn't true and she should be ashamed of herself because I turned out better than what she expected of me, and for that I am grateful. I began to read from the Freedom Writers Diary, *in front of 400 students and the teacher who told me I was stupid. I read, I talked, and I told each of the students to never let anyone tell them they are stupid, worthless, or would not ever graduate. I told them to be who they are and be proud!*

After the presentation was over, students and teachers came up to us and thanked us for coming and sharing stories with their students. While there was a decent size line of students and teachers waiting to talk to us, the one teacher who told me I would amount to nothing was waiting in line to talk to me. I was nervous to hear what she had to say. The conversation started out with a hug (awkward) and ended with "keep up the good work, I always knew you would". After she said that, I was a little angry, but then I realized there is no point to get mad because she is the one who should be angry because her one comment made my middle school experience awful.

I learned a lot through my high school years. I learned to not let people's words affect what you do in life. Be yourself, let yourself decide what you will do with your life. Don't let anyone control it by you. Your life sits in your hands, make of it what you want.

Patrick Brennan (P-Turtle), Student

Sadly, Patrick is one of many who have little self-esteem and confidence. So many young people are battling demons, and by believing in them, those fears fade.

While I have had the pleasure of knowing and loving many students, there are always those few that stand out in your memory because of their personality, their battles, their voice, their innocence, their smile or their victory. Maura Gordon is such a person.

Maura was not a student that cried out for attention. Rather, she sat quietly in the back, mingling with her friends, always the first to ask a question, turn in an assignment, and offer insights to thoughtful discussions. In fact, when we began the research paper process, Maura was eager and excited to learn all that she could. She, by all standards, was a model student. She idolized Celine Dion, was a tremendous athlete, excelling in field hockey, and possessed a smile that would light up the darkest soul. But inside each person lies a story that is waiting to be told, and Maura's story is one that she held as a secret for many, many years.

Maura suffered from a disorder known as Trichotillomania, the compulsive urge to pull out ones hair. I wish I could say I knew this about Maura from day one of meeting her, but, I did not. She hid her disease with utmost secrecy; I had no idea she was coming to school with wigs on each and every day. The bravery she exuded on a daily basis was unimaginable, but I am sure the emotional turmoil playing out in her mind was numbing. She had endured years of ridicule and personal pain; one step forward sometimes created three or four steps back.

It wasn't until she started to write about her

triumphs and defeats, and sharing those words with me, that I was allowed into her secret world. She would come into my room over lunch and discuss the pain, the hurt and the confusion she would be facing on many days. Kids were so cruel and yet Maura continued to smile, hiding the pain from teachers, friends and passersby. To say she was amazing would be an understatement. Being a teenager is a hard enough task - being a teenager with a disorder that is misunderstood is horrible, but being the center of cruel jokes is worse. However, Maura persevered and, with her increased confidence, she began to notice that her disorder was taking a back seat and her hair was slowly returning.

Months passed and one morning Maura showed up at my door. I looked up, said good morning, and went about my work. Instead of Maura coming in, she remained at my door, grinning. I looked up again and that was when I noticed something I will never be ever to erase from my mind. Maura Gordon came to school without a wig! Maura Gordon tackled her condition and came out on top! To say she looked beautiful would be an understatement. Seeing her natural hair, brown and cascading around her shimmering eyes, was a picture forever implanted in my mind. She was glowing and seemed like a completely new person. However, she was shaking more than I realized. I was so proud of her that I did not notice how frightened she really was.

That cold winter morning was the first day of the rest of her life; however, she was about to begin an entire school day with kids "looking" at her, for the first time, without her wig. I could not imagine the fear and the pride that were tangled up inside her soul. All I could do was hug her, cry with her and rejoice with her. Maura Gordon was beginning the first step to freedom and to be a part of that miraculous day was more special than I could ever place into words. She was always beautiful, but that day she was a different kind of beautiful. She possessed poise, grace, promise and happiness intermingled with her outward beauty. She was a new person. She became strong and she was no longer the keeper of a dark secret that she hid from the world. As tears raced down my cheeks, I witnessed Maura turn from my room and walk into the hallway, victorious.

We connected through trust and understanding.

*   *   *

It was my senior year of high school, everyone was worrying about their prom dates, their dress, make-up, their hair style, and most importantly, where they were attending college. I wasn't at all worried about prom; I was worried about getting in to college. I did struggle with academics throughout my life, but like everything else, I figured out how to not let it get in my way of succeeding. Along with stressing out about school, I was struggling day to day with a feisty inner demon that would occasionally win me over. I would make it through an entire day without pulling, but once I would lay down for bed, it felt like I was lying on needles, because of the pain I was in from fighting myself. Most nights, I would cry myself to sleep because I couldn't fight anymore. I am in no way shape or form a loser, but there were some nights I would have to go to bed a loser.

The best way I can explain what it feels like to deal with Trich, is that it feels like a bug bite. You want to itch it so badly, but you know you can't because it is not satisfying the itch. After continuously itching it, you have realized that continuing to itch it for five minutes did not cure anything. That is how I feel day in and day out. I can pull so much so the feeling goes away, but the end result is not positive. So by resisting that itch, the bug bite will fade away. On that same level, if I resist that urge to pull, later on that urge will go away as well.

Trichotillomania is a part of who I am, but it is not completely who I am. Just like everyone else, I have my really good days, and then my really bad days. For me, I have to avoid certain situations that I know are going to cause stress. Yes, this is life, and life comes with stress, but there are certain situations that can be avoided. I had two stress outlets, field hockey and Celine Dion. I would go to my practice or games, and leave everything off the field and play the game that I love. I would also listen to Celine Dion when I was stressed out. Her songs, and her voice was just so calming, and would be put me in a relaxing state of mind. Just like my father always told me, "Everyone has their ways of coping with stress; unfortunately, you deal with yours a little bit differently."

Alongside my family, there has been one person who has had a huge impact on my life. Mrs. Schober was not only my senior year English teacher; she was a role model, and a motherly figure. Mrs. Schober didn't just teach English, she taught us about life, and the obstacles we might run into. She taught a different story to me.

I am not the kind of person who tells everyone what I am going through. Mrs. Schober has an extremely warm heart, and welcoming personality that makes it hard not to talk to her. I finally decided to approach Mrs. Schober and talk to her about what I had been going through for the past eight years. This time, my episodes were getting worse. It was a breath of fresh air to be able to talk to someone who wasn't judging me, or looking down on me.

There would be days when I would be so physically and mentally drained, and not show it, but somehow she knew something was up. She would always squat down right next to my desk and ask how my day was going. I obviously would lie and tell her nothing was wrong. She would give me this look like she knew I was lying.

It was a nice morning during my senior year, when I decided that I was able to take my wig off. I always had long, curly hair, but this time it was short, and really curly. I had extremely bad anxiety that morning; I hesitated about going to school without my wig on. I was scared that people were going to stare at me, and whisper to each other as they passed me in the hallway. Then I snapped out of it, and realized that all my hard work has paid off.

My best friend had picked me up that morning, and that was the longest car ride to school in my life. I had arrived at school a little bit early so that I could show Mrs. Schober before the bell rang. As I approached her room, my heart was racing, wondering what her reaction might be. I saw that she and another teacher were talking, so I stood on the side of her door, and peaked in. She did a double take because didn't realize who I was at first, but when she did, her reaction was priceless. The look on her face was the most amazing look I have ever seen on someone's face before. She came running outside of the door, and immediately hugged me. She was crying, and I was shaking so badly. When she hugged me, it made me feel so good about myself because she was so proud of me. I will never forget that day.

Mrs. Schober has guided me through my senior year of high school, as well as college. I truly believe everything happens for a reason because I was placed in her English class for a reason. I believe the reason why I was placed in her classroom was that she has taught me what it is to be strong, independent, and smart. She has also encouraged me to open up, and get my story out there.

Mrs. Schober has always helped me strive to be my very best. It is an amazing feeling to have a teacher who truly cares about her students, even after we have graduated high school. If it wasn't for Mrs. Schober, I don't think I would have made it through my senior year, or be the independent, strong and knowledgeable person that I am today. She has forever made a footprint on my heart.

Maura Gordon, Student

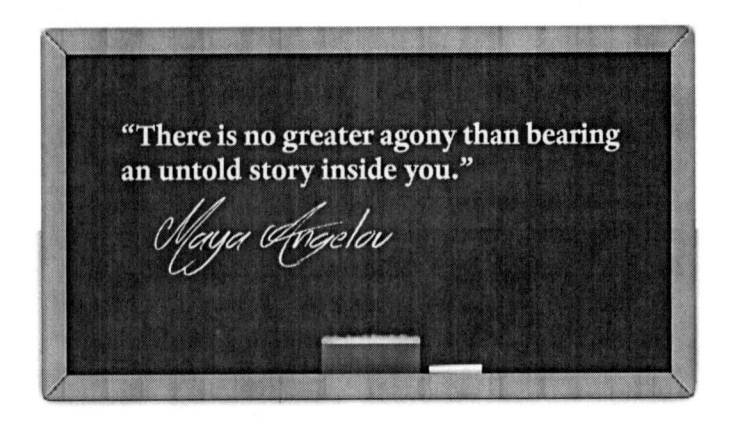

> "There is no greater agony than bearing an untold story inside you."
>
> *Maya Angelou*

SECRET INGREDIENT #2
BREAK DOWN COMFORT ZONES

Students from different schools, ethnicities, economic and religious backgrounds, sexual orientations... how do you get them to understand that each has a story and each person has something in common with someone else... we are the same, yet different?

Teaching about Shakespeare, Chaucer, O'Brien, Carver, Joyce and other prominent authors is easy. But, how do you raise the comfort level and get to really the know the students, and, in the meantime, help them to know each other? Why is it even important?

When I was in California, the second day of our institute was filled with tears. We went from fun and games to intense learning moments of which I was not prepared. The one activity that challenged me on many levels was the Line Game. We walked into a classroom where the desks were pushed off to the sides of the room and there was a line of tape drawing a division in the classroom. We were instructed to stand on either side of the tape and to step up to the line when the question asked was relevant to us. To my left and right, I was surrounded by new friends, original Freedom Writer students, and teachers who I had yet to connect with. I felt comfortable, yet alienated. I was unsure of what to expect, but I knew I needed to trust.

Erin quickly began spurting out one statement after another...

"Step to the line if you like to dance."

"Step to the line if you have been to the beach."

What started as fun and frolic, quickly turned into the most emotional moment I have ever experienced.

"Step to the line if you have ever lost a loved one to cancer."

"Step to the line if you know someone who has been asked to join a gang."

"Step to the line if you know someone who has been raped."

With that last question, my heart stopped. Do I step to the line? Do I, in front of all these "strangers", admit that I have been raped? Do I become vulnerable, risking a breakdown? After what seemed like hours, I slowly stepped up to the line. I looked to my right; no one was there. I looked to my left and noticed one other person standing on the line with me. I was safe.

The Line Game brought a group of random teachers from throughout the United States together. We learned what we had in common; we learned of hardships, triumphs, and setbacks. If this could work with a group of adults, surely this would work with my students.

The first time I used the Line Game in the class-

-room was with my freshman Academic Skills class, The Mix. I wanted them to see the bonds they shared with each other. I wanted them to grow as a family, and they did. In fact, they asked to do the Line Game at least once a week! But, how would my seniors react to this activity? We were beginning the craziest time of year, college essay writing, and I needed them to trust each other so that they could share their most intimate writing. I picked the day. I was nervous, hoping they wouldn't think of this activity as a joke.

As the seniors came into the room, they noticed the tape dividing their once orderly desks. A lot of questions were being thrown in my direction, but I simply smiled and ignored their curious antics. The bell rang and they looked at me with questioning glances. I showed them a clip from the *Freedom Writer* movie, where Erin and her students were doing the Line Game, and they got excited.

"Are we going to do this?" was asked over and over again.

"Yes", I eagerly replied.

We pushed the desks to the side of the room and each of them took their spots on either side of the tape. I began with the easy questions and the laughter and jokes were contagious. They challenged each other to dance moves when I questioned their dancing skills. They laughed when football players stood on the line because they owned a Back Street Boys CD. And then... I smacked them with the hard questions. One by one, the seniors became somber, searching for others who witnessed gun shots, violence and lost loved ones to disease. The room became silent and a few tears exposed their innocence. I remember being overwhelmed at their honesty, openness and trust. I decided to take it one step further. I turned to the seniors and opened the questions up to them. If they wanted to ask a question, this was their chance. There was silence. And, then... I heard one faint voice followed by another, and then another...

"Step to the line if you have ever cut yourself."

"Step to the line if you feel you have disappointed your parents."

"Step to the line if you have done something you regret."

"Step to the line if you drank this weekend."

I stood in awe as I witnessed the trust overflowing in front of me. When silence once again filled the room, I instructed the students to walk quietly back to their desks and take out their journals and I quietly asked them:

"What did you learn today that you didn't know before the class started? About yourself? About others?"

The class was quiet and the writing did not stop. I was witnessing something I never thought possible... I was witnessing solidarity. They were a group now... a bond was forming... a trust was evolving. It was time to write, share, and continue growing.

We connected through the power of breaking down comfort zones in order to expose our real selves.

Tears, tears, and more tears! Mouth wide open, heart breaking! That was my first memory of the "LINE GAME".

"If you want to teach the kids, I mean really teach them, you've got to get to know them. And I mean really know them – their joys, their sorrows, their successes, their failures, their love, and their hurt." I'm not sure that these were Anne's exact words, but they are awfully close to what she told me when she invited me into her classroom to observe an activity she called the "Line Game." Step to the line if ....

At first it was really simple. Step to the line if you have a brother or sister; or, step to the line if you went to the beach this summer; or, step to the line if you plan on going to college when you graduate high-school. Lots of laughs and comments from the students – "Wish I was an only child", "Wish I had a brother or sister", "Oh yeah, and did I ever meet a hot guy/girl", "Penn State, Notre Dame, Temple," etc.

Then things got real serious: "Step to the line if you know somebody who has been arrested"; "Step to the line if you have been arrested"; "Step to the line if you know somebody who has died from a drug overdose"; "Step to the line if you know somebody who has been shot"; Step to the line if you have been a victim of sexual abuse"; "Step to the line if you have been raped";

"Step to the line ...."

And the kids stepped to the line, sometimes just one, sometimes two, sometimes most of the class. My heart pounded, I felt short of breath, the tears flowed. I was witnessing something I didn't know how to handle. I was witnessing a moment of trust that I had never seen before among student and teacher(s). To be a part of that moment was humbling, it was sorrowful, it was a blessing. It opened my eyes to "teaching."

Anne was able to reach her students at their very core.

She developed a trusting relationship that allowed the students to share their very selves, from their greatest joys and aspirations to their very deepest hurts and regrets. She loved her students and from what I observed on that very day, they loved her. Loved her more than she or I could ever imagine. I wanted that, I wanted that level of trust, I wanted to be just like her with my students.

Teaching isn't just a book with facts and figures – teaching is developing a relationship with your students at the very deepest level. Everything after that is "icing on the cake."

Jim Rogers, Teacher

✷   ✷   ✷

My final year of high school is not one that can be measured by time; simply impossible to be measured by the "ticks" of the clock hanging high on the wall nor by the finely grated sand sifting its way through an hour glass. My final year of high school, my favorite English I had ever taken in the past four years, can be measured only by the everyday laughter, the rare salty tears, the abundant smiles, and life-lasting memories.

A year full of lessons will be a year never forgotten. From all the books we read, all the movies we witnessed and all the short stories discussed, the lesson I found most interesting was how unique every student was that had an enormous impact on me. It was not a discussion, rather, a game. The Line Game.

After watching The Freedom Writers *multiple times and seeing change in the faces of the participants, I could not help but wish to play this lesson-filled game. Not only once, but twice did the opportunity present itself to me. Both times, once in the classroom and once in the school parking lot with a visiting middle school, I discovered not only something new about a classmate or friend, but found new light within myself. Through remembering old memories that were once washed away and forgotten, or finally being completely with myself, I grew from each moment and question and left a better person to myself and to others. The Line Game helped to give me courage to not only know myself better but also to grow to know others better.*

In growing to learn to understand others better, a single piece of literature caused me to open my eyes to the truth of pain, guilt, sorrow and redemption. The Kite Runner *hit me harder than any other book I have read. From the beginning, I had negative thoughts like "Why this book?", "I hate these kinds of books", "This is going to be a complete waste of time". Then, slowly, I felt sorrow and anger toward the characters and I tried to gain as much as I could from the words. I learned about redemption and the steps needed to give another a better life. And I learned the importance of planting a smile on another's face. I did one of the worst possible things to this book before I even got to read it – I judged it. The one lesson Mrs. Schober dedicated this year to and I did the exact opposite within half the year. But, I learned from it. I learned that nothing in this world has a less importance to anything else in this world. I changed.*

I have grown into a great young man and know I am only going to continue to grow. I have learned that I am surrounded by those who care and that I am never alone. I have learned that my mother is looking down on me with a smile beaming from her face because she is proud and loves me still. I learned to become a better friend and put others before me. I continue to grow and plan on living this lifestyle for the remainder of my life. I plan on changing this world, making the world see the importance of a smile for everyone to know that they are not alone. "Darkness cannot expel darkness, only light can do that. Hate cannot expel hate, only love can do that." Martin Luther King Jr. wrote those words and until this year in Senior English class, they were merely words. It took a class like this to show me the true meaning.

Matt Pleger, Student

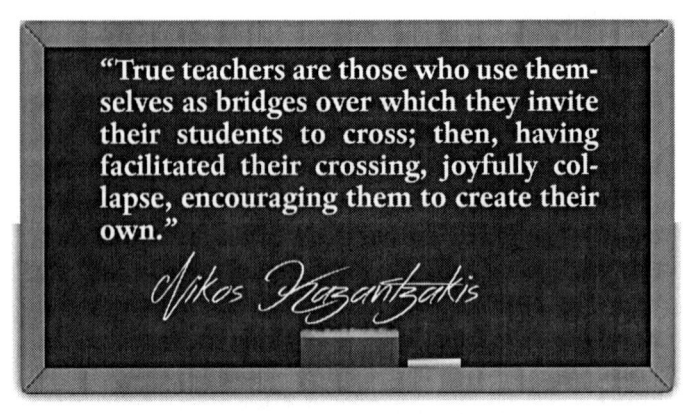

> "True teachers are those who use themselves as bridges over which they invite their students to cross; then, having facilitated their crossing, joyfully collapse, encouraging them to create their own."
>
> *Nikos Kazantzakis*

SECRET INGREDIENT #3
Establish a Safe Environment

A few years ago, I was asked to attend a workshop on Restorative Justice, a unique and inclusive way of practicing discipline within a school environment where the victims took an active role in the process and offenders were encouraged to take responsibility for their actions. It allowed for all involved in the incident to have a voice and to help the perpetrator to understand how his/her actions affected others. As part of the process, all involved sat in a circle and held an honest conversation with those included and affected. It was eye-opening and showed fast results. I decided to take this concept and incorporate it into my classroom.

"Circle it up" was a phrase I said over and over each day. In fact, most students would walk into Room 123 and immediately began pushing their desks into circle formation. I loved being able to look at each student as they spoke and I felt it allowed for more comfort and acceptance. We would use the circle to peer edit writing pieces, discuss themes found in our literature study and even to discover how the day was going. But the circle had another advantage: it allowed the students to face each other and gain greater acceptance. Some days, students walked in and requested a circle because they had something they needed to discuss. Other days, I would request a circle so that we could peer edit a writing piece, have a discussion on stereotypes, and other relevant topics or activities. It was working with my Project Based Learning classes where the circle became an integral part of the classroom.

The students in Project Based Learning were a combination of general, Academic and Honors learners. They were a vast array of eclectic opposites. It was important for me to establish a safe classroom where everyone felt accepted, safe, and understood. The class bonded through the Line Game, Toast for Change, People Bingo, and simple talks that sometimes went beyond the sound of the bell. Why did I take time out of the curriculum to get to know my students on a more personal level? Because you cannot teach about Shakespeare, Joyce or teach the research process if the students are not clear of mind and invested in learning. I showed my students that I was devoted to them so that they would be invested in what I knew needed to be taught. It was a common occurrence where a student would apologize if they did not do their homework or felt they did not do their best on test. They showed they cared not just about their learning experience, but about others, as well. I knew it was time to dig deeper and for them to understand they each have a story, they each have a voice, they each deserved to be heard. What began as a writing exercise quickly became a life changing experience for the students and myself.

It was a cold, rather dreary morning when I asked

the class to circle it up and have their journals out on their desk. We were in the beginning phases of choosing our project for the year, and the students were still in their comfortable worlds, not willing to go beyond their comfort zone of friends. I asked each student to answer the following prompt: "If you really knew me, you would know…" The writing that ensued lasted the entire period; they did not want to stop writing! It was inspiring to see reluctant writers writing! I had no idea what to expect, but what happened next was truly miraculous. The students were asking to read their entries! Even as the bell rang, and they clamored into the hallway, I could hear them saying to one another, "I want to share my entry, too!" "I can't believe how fast that class period went!" They wanted to share themselves with the class, but I knew that we had to set boundaries. I needed them to know that if any of them divulged something that I thought was dangerous to themselves or someone else, I needed to report it to guidance. Their safety was my utmost concern and I would do anything to keep them safe.

What they revealed opened my eyes to a reality that I did not want to face but I knew there was no turning back. No one has a "perfect" life, but my students were suffering in unimaginable ways. No wonder some of them were failing! How could they go home and do homework when they were responsible for the care of the house? How could they worry about school work when they faced abuse at the hands of those who "loved" them? As each of them shared their stories, I knew that nothing would ever be the same…

We connected through acceptance.

*   *   *

What started out seeming like the worst day ever, turned out to be one of the greatest experiences of my life. I walked into room 123, a place where I always felt at home. I had been having troubles at home and I had already been in a car accident that morning. Walking into that room I was already feeling more vulnerable than ever. We had been in the process of telling our stories as a way of getting to know our Communications class better. Mrs. Schober thought it would be a good time to share my story considering the circumstances.

I started to tell my story and I couldn't even make it through a sentence without crying. I spoke of tragic childhood memories that I had never spoken of before. I was afraid everyone would judge me and think of me differently, but as I looked around, people were crying and showing looks of great sympathy. They felt for me and they truly cared. Nobody judged me and they were all there for me.

After I finished, every single person in the class hugged me and told me how strong I was and how they admired me. Some people even said they knew what I was going through and that felt so good. I was not alone anymore. This day marked a new beginning for our class. It made us see we could trust each other and it truly brought us all closer together. After I told my story, it helped other people in my class come out and say their story. That day will forever be embedded in my head and will always be a day that changed me for the better.

Katie Filling, Student

If you really knew me you would know that I am most afraid of being alone, not having anyone there for me to love, be with, or even talk to. You would know that I really love and enjoy music! I listen to it every day, all the time, and I really LOVE to dance. Whenever I hear music, I cannot help but move to the beat. Whenever I listen to music it makes me forget about everything that is going on around me. Sometimes it even helps me find myself when I am feeling lost. Music and dancing... you can never go wrong with those two!

I remember when I fell in love for the first time, it was a feeling I never felt before and I did not want it to go away. It felt so right and so DAMN good. He was such a great and loving guy; we had so much fun when we were together. We would crack jokes, mess around in class and get in trouble; we would even stay up late texting. He was my knight, my king, and my baby and everything I always wanted in a guy. I always asked myself how we ended up together. We were so different and never hung out at all, but when you are in love, none of that matters. As long as you have that one person, life is good. But then things started to change between us. We stopped texting, talking... everything just stopped. I was confused on what was going on between us; we were slowly fading away. I started doing my own thing and he did his. Everything between us just went downhill and it went even more downhill when I did some crazy, stupid things that I regret. If I had not done those things, I would still have him. Now he is with someone else and that is just something I am going to have deal with, knowing that I am never going to have what I once had, but lost. We are still great friends, but I am never going to love another like I loved him. He was my king, my jackass, my love and my life.

If you really knew me, you would know that the relationships I have with my family are not the greatest.

A lot of the time there are arguments and bad things being said. I am closest with my dad. We do a lot of things together; I like to call them "Daddy and Daughter Day". Here and there I may bump heads with my sister and brothers, I mean that IS what brothers and sisters do, but at the end of the day I love my family very much. I just wish things would get better. In due time it will because God does not give us more than we can bear.

If you really knew me you would know that I am not close with anyone. I tell certain people certain things about me, but I leave the important and serious things out. I can really trust my English teacher, but I am just not ready to reveal the true and real me. I know she won't judge me nor look at me differently. I am just not ready.

If you really knew me you would know that I wish I could go back in time and change all the bad to GOOD, but then I think to myself if I change the bad to good then what would I have to grow stronger from? I wouldn't be wiser...hell, I wouldn't be the person I am today. Sometimes you just have to roll the dice to get somewhere in life, be who you are and love who you are, have no regrets and life for the moment and cherish the memories. I really do not regret much or some things I did, I just regret the timing everything happened and took place. But there is one thing I do regret and that is not telling my family what happened to me.

If you really knew me you would know that I cannot forget the time I lost my virginity or the time I was raped and being depressed for long periods of time. I try not to think about it; I just bury it deep down inside and try to move on. I forgive the person, but I will never forget. I have become a very strong and independent person and I will not let the negative things in my past get me down. I will find someone to love me for all of me and the person I will grow to become.

*Chloe (name changed), Student

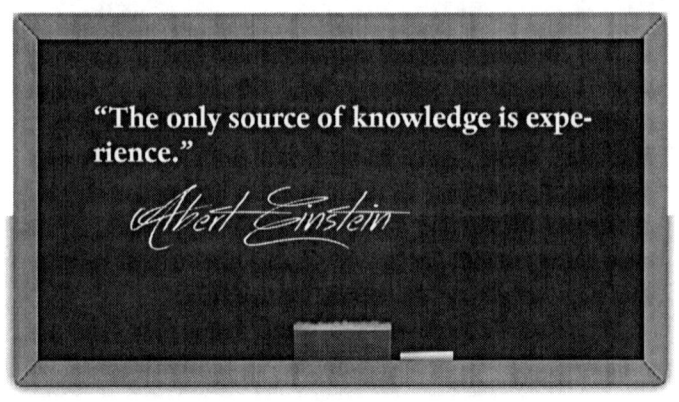

> "The only source of knowledge is experience."
>
> *Albert Einstein*

SECRET INGREDIENT #4
Validate Prior Knowledge

I avoided the faculty lounge. I remember the first time I went "down to the trenches" and thought how awesome it was to have lunch in the same room where, as students, we imagined what was behind those sacred doors. It was simply a room filled with heavenly aromas and fellow faculty chatting about their weekends, their families and the latest vacation plans. But that was the unusual. Most times you would hear faculty members complaining about John Smith, Jane Doe, and all the other students that they are teaching throughout the day. I tried to avoid these conversations, but one day I just had to step in. They were bashing on "one of my" kids and I was becoming more angry as the conversation continued.

"He does nothing but give me one excuse after another and then, when I tell him I don't have time for his excuses, he goes back to his desk and doesn't even try the rest of the class. One time he asked me how to do the most basic of math problems and I laughed at him. I thought that would make him try harder", said one teacher.

"That is how he is in my class, too," complained yet another teacher, "except he throws in several swear words and makes a scene before I make him leave."

By this time, my heart was pounding and my face was becoming red with frustration. I had to speak up.

"This student you are talking about is going through a lot right now. His cousin just died and his father is an alcoholic. He goes home to a war zone. He does not have time to finish his work, let alone understand what was taught to him in school because when he gets home he feels he needs to protect his mother and sister from his dad. He doesn't understand why his cousin had to die so suddenly. He is angry at the world. Maybe if you took the time to figure out what was going on with him instead of brushing it off, you would understand where he is coming from and what is going on in his life. Learning about math and science do not matter to him right now when his life is nothing but turmoil. Maybe when he comes in to your classroom tomorrow you could ask how he is before belittling him in front of the class."

I turned, walked out the door, and never returned. Some may think by not returning that I was not there to "speak up" for my kids, but, in reality, it did not change anything. I discovered that if a teacher does not like a student from the beginning, they will likely never change their attitude. I was approached by other teachers who discussed with me students they had as freshmen who "did not perform to their abilities", and was told not to expect much from them in my classroom. Other teachers would discuss former students' "bad behaviors" and "poor writing" skills. I chose not to listen. My philosophy was really quite simple: "New year, new you." I never listened to negative criticism in regards to a student; that would be unfair to them and to me. Instead, I stayed away from such statements and kept to myself by staying in my room and having lunch with my students and my thoughts. It was a much better way to spend my time.

By doing this, I quickly learned more about my students than I could have ever imagined. I learned of their home life, their social life, and everything in between. I learned their stories and was able to offer some "motherly" advice when asked. I also learned that many of my students were more intelligent than what was stated on their report cards at the end of each quarter. They understood life and all the good and bad that made it challenging. They, in their short eighteen years, had been exposed to more than I would ever want. Instead of shying away from these circumstances, I learned to embrace each one and connect them to literature and writing in any way possible. When a student had an issue with bullying, we would discuss it in-depth while reading the *Kite Runner* or *Catcher in the Rye*. I took what they knew and capitalized on their expertise. If they felt comfortable, many of our circle conversations would be led by the expert of the topic, giving them leadership and confidence in a world that sometimes took their self-esteem away.

We connected because I cared.

✶   ✶   ✶

What I learned in Mrs. Schober's class surpasses anything I had learned before that and every other class I have taken since. Yes, we learned about writing. Yes, we learned about grammar. But the lessons went beyond and above that.

I learned that I am not the only one who has struggled with rape. Being able to see that someone like Mrs. Schober, kind, caring, beautiful, and intelligent, can be what she is after her past was inspiring. I use to have thoughts such as, "no one could ever understand me" and "no one knows what I am going through." But along with teaching me that both of those thoughts were completely false, she showed that I am not what happened to me. I am not my mistakes, I am not my fears, and because I of her I was able to truly be comfortable in my skin. She is a successful woman with all her mistakes behind her. I have learned to be the same way.

I have learned to be myself totally and completely. I am not ashamed of who I am, what happened to me, or what I have been through. I am proud of it and I embrace it. I have learned to put my trust in God, and to not mind what other people say. I could continue with the curriculum of Night *or* Catcher in the Rye *but I don't think either of those books taught me anything close to what she did. Mrs. Schober, this could not even begin to explain the life lessons you have taught me. But for now it will have to do.*

Abbey Patterson, Student

I will never look at an English teacher the same. I have had some pretty incredible English teachers, but none of them will ever, or have ever, lived up the PAR that Mrs. Anne Schober has set. No teacher can be your best friend, role model, and advocator as well as Mrs. Schober has. She turns the classroom into an open field of adventure. An adventure that will tug on your heartstrings, piss you off, and make you embrace your worst enemy with open arms.

I had Mrs. Schober 6th period. That was right after lunch. Which meant the period after you got in on the latest gossip. If you know anything about me, it is that I despise drama. I mean, who gives a shit about some chick who hooked up with your ex-boyfriend. Anyway, most days went like that in high school. You drowsily roll out of bed way too late, drive 30 miles over the speed limit just to get there in time, listen to monotonous lectures, go to a rigorous sport practice, do your five hours of homework, get some well-earned sleep just to wake up and do it all again. That all changed the first time I stepped into Mrs. Schober's English class.

The first words she said were, "this is your classroom, not mine. You can sit on the floor, write wherever you like, take books as you please. Do what you want, this is your place." I wish I could use words to describe the reaction on my face. I was pleasantly perplexed. As class went on, I quickly knew this was going to be my favorite class.

Throughout the year we were assigned things that every English teacher assigns: read this book, write this paper, let's build a resume. Things of that nature. But, the difference was the way these assignments were discussed. We didn't take tests on Jo Shmo's book on Slugs and study our eyes out to fill in bubbles on a scantron sheet (that was not an actual book nor author, by the way). Mrs. Schober turned her classroom into a debate room where a "disagree," sign and an, "agree," sign were placed on opposite sides of the room. When we disagreed or agreed with a statement relevant to the book, we stepped to that side and explained ourselves. Sometimes we would only get through one question because they were that controversial.

Another thing that Mrs. Schober did really well was help you to figure out where your life has been, if you are okay with that, and are you okay with where your life is going. It didn't stop there. If we weren't okay with any of those three things, she would miraculously help us to change them. She did all of this through teaching us how to be incredible writers.

One day we walked into class and all the desks were pushed against the walls and there was a long line of tape on the floor. Mrs. Schober had us all stand on either sides of the line. She had a list of questions, both serious and non-serious. She would ask questions like, "who in here thinks they are a good dancer?" If you thought you were a good dancer, you stepped to the line. But some questions were like, "have you lost someone to suicide?" And if you did, you stepped to the line. You can imagine the amount of tears that were secretly shed that day. Tears for our own sorrow and tears for our classmates - even the girls that gossiped.

We wrote about our lives, our heroes, tough times and joyful times. We learned to have a remarkable amount of respect for every person in the world because God only knows what they are going through right now. That was the other thing about Mrs. Schober... She never let a bad incident at home, in school, or in her family jeopardize making someone else's life better. This woman was going through a tremendous amount of difficulties, yet she managed to be in class and talk about **hard** *things. She would never miss an opportunity to make someone else's life easier to get by.*

I had the amazing opportunity to be with Mrs. Schober

more than just during sixth period. I was the president of an incredible club called Aevidum. It is a word made up of Latin roots that literally means, "I've got your back." We raised awareness for teen suicide and depression and man was that heart changing.

My senior year of high school my sister was struggling with depression. One day, she texted me during first period and said, "Kayla, my friends saw the cuts on my arm because I left my sweater at home, can I borrow your sweater?" I did not even know that my sister was back to cutting at this point. So, my shock and fear after reading that text during my physics class was as sharp as a blade being punctured through my heart. The first place I went was Mrs. Schober's room.

"Emily just texted me that these kids saw her wrist and she needs my sweater and I don't know where she is. What do I do? Oh my goodness," I was sobbing. I was lucky to even get that pushed out of my lungs, through my mouth, and into her ears.

"Kayla, relax," Mrs. Schober said as she grabbed my shoulders, "we will find her right now and get her a sweater." A huge gasp was released from my body. I must have been holding my breath for a long time. Before I knew it, Mrs. Schober had my sister and me talking one-on-one calming each other down. Emily had a sweater to wear and promised to try and stop cutting. All in a matter of two hours, this woman had completely flopped my day around. Miraculous is an understatement.

Later in the year, the day before prom to be exact, my best friend's ex-boyfriend texted me a picture of my friends wrist slit open. He said that she was threatening to take her life. I had spent that night awake, calling our group of friends letting them know what was happening. One of us stayed in contact with Michelle*, one of us called Michelle's sister, and the others tried to get Michelle's ex-

-boyfriend to stop texting her. I, on the other hand, immediately called Mrs. Schober. I told her what was happening and she knew exactly what to say, "Kayla, get someone in her house to go to her room and stay there. If you girls need to go over, do that as soon as possible. Stay calm and we all will have a meeting first thing tomorrow morning."

That is exactly how things went. Michelle went to Phil Haven (a mental and behavioral hospital) the next morning. Her parents were notified and were relieved that Michelle had friends that would be so willing to send her away for a while in order to save her life. I was so lucky to have had Mrs. Schober. If it weren't for Mrs. Schober, Michelle would have never gone to Phil Haven and gotten better. She never would have gained back all the weight she had lost. She never would have gone to college, or got her new puppy. Michelle very well could be dead.

So, when I say that Mrs. Schober saved lives, I wasn't kidding. If she didn't save your life, she changed it, and that very well could be the same thing. This woman is not called Mrs. Schober by me anymore, she called Momma Schober. I am still in contact with Momma Schober and I can guarantee that I always will be. She has been such a blessing in my life as well as to my friends, and family. She will do much more than teach you what a transition is - she will teach you what success is. And like *Ralph Waldo Emerson* said, "To know that a life has breathed easier because you have lived - that is to have succeed," Momma Schober exemplifies. She will teach you that life is about giving and through this giving you will gain.

Thank you Momma Schober for teaching me that life will curve down very low paths but it will always go back up mountains to see a beautiful view.

Kayla Leed, 18, Student, Brevard, NC

* indicates a name change to maintain the persons anonymity

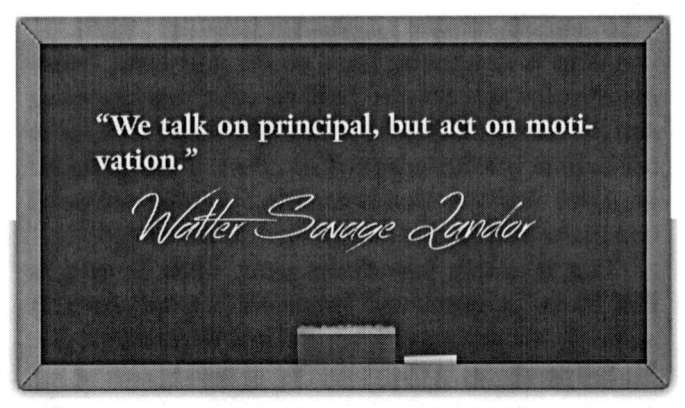

> "We talk on principal, but act on motivation."
>
> *Walter Savage Landor*

SECRET INGREDIENT #5
MOTIVATE YOUR STUDENTS

If you could change the world, what would you do? That one question changed the format of my classroom and, in turn, changed the lives of many.

After having some of my students for three years in a row, I knew the curriculum they were being taught was not beneficial to their future plans. It was not because they were considered "lower level"; they learned differently and I knew it was necessary to rethink why we teach what we teach and to whom we teach it. Why do some students need to know Shakespeare when they are going into the armed services? Why do others need to learn about Hemingway and Carver when they are going to a trade school to learn mechanics? While I believe that the classics are informative and allow a glimpse into the worlds' most renowned authors, sometimes we, as educators, are setting our students up for failure. That was when I decided I needed to make a change in the English curriculum. After much research and brainstorming with another English teacher, Leslie Laird, we proposed Service/Project Based Learning to our administration. We went into the meeting with eyes wide open and eagerness in our hearts. We came out of the meeting with a new class in our hands! We began to get to work.

When my Mix students walked into Room 123 on their first day of their senior year, they were excited and nervous about our upcoming year. This year was going to be different and I was going to challenge them more than they ever thought possible. I handed them the syllabus which gave an overview of the course. I waited, searching their eyes for their responses.

"Wait, we are going to do a project that is going to last the whole year?"

"What are we going to do?"

"This is going to be awesome!"

It was time to get to work. We started with the small questions and eventually approached the harder question which centered the entire classroom experience.

"In your notebooks, respond to the following questions:

1. If you could change anything in the school, what would it be and why? Would you want air conditioning? Shorter school days? Less rules?

2. If you could change anything in your own community, what would you change? Would you ask for more police presence? Would you want more activities for teens?

3. If you could change anything in the state of Pennsylvania, what would you change? Would you lower taxes? Work on the unemployment rates?

4. If you could change anything in the United States, what would you change? Do not limit yourself... think big!"

Prior to the class period ending, I informed the students that they needed to go home and interview their parents and family and ask them the same questions, but concentrate mostly on the last one. They were also asked to interview their teachers and fellow students and get their ideas, as well. They had their assignment and could not wait to begin.

They came into class the next day and immediately began recounting the answers they discovered. They shared their responses and the discussion was lively and engaging. And then, I hit them with the big question: "If you could change the world, what would you do?" Immediately, their hands went up in the air.

"I think we should do something for the Freedom Writers Foundation. They have helped us for the past four years, we should do something for them!"

"Yea, we should! I like that idea!"

Immediately I witnessed The Mix coming together to unite on one cause. They discussed their ideas with each other, as well as researched different options. They came to a unanimous decision: "We want to go to California, work at a teenage runaway shelter and fix up the Freedom Writers Foundation office as a complete surprise and a "thank you" for all they have done for us!" My heart melted as I saw the motivation and passion in their eyes.

They immediately got to work and constructed a business plan, made contacts in Los Angeles, searched for places to stay and looked into flight plans. Every single day in the classroom was spent finalizing plans and working together to make this project happen. We accomplished a lot, but we had one major hurdle to conquer: We had to ask administration for their blessing. We put together a power point with all the information we had gathered and practiced, practiced and practiced until the presentation was professional and the kids were confident.

The day came and the kids were excited. They presented their project to the administration with all related expenses and waited for a response. The answer was "No." We were not allowed to travel to California. Because of recent national issues, the Diocese wouldn't allow groups to travel beyond a certain boundary. California was not within the limits. I saw their hearts breaking in front of me. Their passion was slowly leaving them and I had to do something, quick.

"What is the farthest distance of where we can travel?"

The principal looked at the students, then at me and said, "I will be able to grant you a 600 mile radius. But it cannot be any more than that. And you will have to drive."

"Okay, you have a deal!"

After our meeting, The Mix pulled up a map of the United States on the Smart Board, put a dot on Lancaster and drew a circle with a circumference to match our limited mileage. A hundred miles outside our circumference sat Nashville, Tennessee, a place that was ravaged by floods in May of their junior year. We had watched the devastation play out on national television and when we discussed this as a possibility, the kids were starting to get excited again. Because I did not want them to be disheartened again, as soon as they left the classroom I went to meet with my principal and asked if we could travel to Nashville to help those affected by the flooding. Without hesitation he answered "Yes". Nashville was our new destination and it was time to get a plan of action together.

Over the following months, the kids were consistently busy. Our double periods together went by quickly and we needed to meet more than just during school hours. Some days we stayed after school, other days we met over lunch, and we sometimes met on weekends to get everything together. We decided that we wanted to help a school which had been affected by the flooding and do whatever they needed. We made countless phone calls and no one was interested in our help. Our hearts were deflating. But, we didn't give up. I got in touch with a professor at Vanderbilt, Dr. Barbara Stengel, who was a friend of the family, and asked her to think of schools that could use our help. She immediately gave us the names of two schools and that is how we learned of Kirkpatrick Enhanced Option Elementary School. While it was not affected by the flooding, it needed help. Their family's average annual income was a mere $5,000. Rain or shine, the kids walked to school in worn shoes without umbrellas or raincoats. This is where we needed to go. This is where we wanted to help.

We made several phone calls to the school and finally got in touch with the principal, Ms. Moorman, and we assured her this was not a joke.... We wanted to do whatever they needed. We would paint walls, purchase school supplies, desks, clothing, shoes, build a playground, anything they needed. We asked them to put together a "wish list" and we began our campaign of letter writing and business presentations so that we could make their dreams come true. We built a powerful power point presentation and video which accompanied us on our visits to possible donors. We spoke in front of the school board, to presidents of Banks, business firms, individuals and many more. At the end of four long, intensive months, we had raised over $16,000!

We called Kirkpatrick and informed them that we would be painting their school, build a teachers lounge for the overworked educators, erect a playground and bring a truckload of clothes, furniture, and school supplies. They were shocked, ecstatic and full of smiles and appreciation. We were going to change their world!

Before we left for Nashville, Erin Gruwell came to wish "The Mix" a bon voyage, but she did so in true "Erin-style." She spoke before the entire school, encouraging them all to change what needed to be changed, whether it was something within their own hearts or the community at large. She called "The Mix" kids in front of the entire school and praised them for their compassion, work ethic, love and empathy for those who are less fortunate. She expressed her love and support for them as they were ready to embark on journey that would not only change the lives in Nashville, Tennessee, but would change their own lives forever. With tears, kisses and hugs, "The Mix" was sent off with a lavish farewell and words of confidence from their role model, hero, and inspiration.... Erin Gruwell.

We connected through our motivation to help others.

"You're taking them where?" I asked.

"Nashville", she said.

"And, we're going to raise $20,000 to build a playground", she continued.

"Oh, OK", I understood.

As Anne Schober's husband, I understood that once she got an idea in her head, it was going to happen. Even though there were hundreds of details to be worked out, she trusted that someone somewhere would provide the means, the answer or the direction she needed. I understood that the possibility of her group not going to Nashville was not an option. And so I watched in the following weeks and months as her group of students methodically worked their plan to raise money and work out the logistics of the trip. I was impressed with the focus and determination of each person as they slowly advanced their plan.

Of course I got conscripted to drive the U-Haul to Nashville and to figure out how to layout and install the playground. I thought the assignment to the U-Haul was great because I wasn't in the van with eight crazy, excited and overly-stimulated teenagers for 12 hours! Fortunately, we broke-up the trip with a stop in West Virginia so Anne and her students could perform a seminar on the Freedom Writer program for some local teachers. Again, not only was Anne engaging, but her students quickly earned the attention and respect of the seminar attendees.

We arrived at Kirkpatrick the next day and the kids were greeted like rock stars. It was amazing to see Anne's students immediately bond with the students from Kirkpatrick. I was concerned that this would become a distraction to Anne's students given the significant amount of work that needed to be done. But, as usual, the kids came through and were very focused as they painted, cleaned, stock shelves and created a welcome mural. Fortunately, we were able to work over the weekend while the

Kirkpatrick students were at home. But come Monday, there were plenty of smiling faces and excited Kirkpatrick students.

At one point, Anne and I had to go to Lowes to pick up thirty 80-pound bags of concrete mix for the playground. It was one of the few opportunities we had to be alone and we enjoyed the quiet time together. That quickly came to an end when someone at Lowes recognized Anne from a previous evening news report on our trip (it's not easy being married to a famous person)!

The next day we installed the playground, mixed 2,400 pounds of concrete and moved a mountain of mulch. We also had to return the U-Haul which meant I had to drive the van home with all the overly-stimulated teens close behind! Fortunately, everyone was completely exhausted from all the hard work that most everyone slept or relaxed during the trip while Anne and I took turns driving.

It was really an awesome trip. Not because of what these kids accomplished, but rather because of the way in which they accomplished it. They were very focused on the project and committed to its success. They impressed a lot of people and made some lifelong friendships in the process.

Mike Schober, Husband

After being together for three years, our fourth year was starting and we all wanted to go out with a bang. We put our heads together and came up with a plan to travel over 500 miles to help people in need. After weeks of researching a place in need we finally chose Kirkpatrick Elementary School located in Nashville, Tennessee. Kirkpatrick needed our help in a big way and, after talking to the principal, we learned many things about the school and its students including the average annual income for the families was $5,000, many children were going to school without breakfast and returning home without dinner on the table, they were walking to school on rainy days without any way to keep dry, and they were growing up and living in a bad neighborhood. In addition to the problems that the children were facing, we were also notified about problems that faced the faculty. The faculty were struggling to maintain office and school supplies in the classroom, they were without proper tools to keep a classroom running, and the children were without physical education toys, did not have a playground to play on, and were without a lounge to debrief in and interact with their fellow co-workers.

After hearing this directly from the principal, we all decided that this was the place we needed to help and in a big way. With the help from our teacher, Anne Schober, we came up with our plan which included how much money we needed to raise, how we were going to travel, and a list of the supplies we wanted to purchase. After days of intense planning we decided that we wanted to raise over $20,000 purchase office supplies, physical education equipment, building the children a playground, paint the school hallways, build a mural, and build the teachers a new lounge.

We started planning this trip in August and the trip was in April, which didn't give us a lot of time to get this together. We started coming up with ways to fundraise *which included a car wash, bake sale, making public presentations, sending out letters to our family and friends and selling Valentines flowers inside the school to try and reach $20,000.*

During the months of planning we got in contact with many people who were generous enough to donate money to our trip, we were handed boxes upon boxes of school supplies, and with our remaining money we put it towards buying a playground set, making a new lounge, and buying paint for the school hallways. We were ready to go!

April 14, 2011

Having packed all morning and sleeping very little due to excitement, we are ready to embark on our journey to Nashville, TN. With Mr. Schober driving the U-Haul and Mrs. Schober driving the 12-passenger van, they finally arrived at school an hour late. There were a lot of students to help us load all the school supplies, carpets, clothes, backpacks, books and so much more. After almost an hour of loading, we said our goodbyes to our family and friends and we were on our way! Our first stop was only two hours away...Martinsburg, West Virginia. We arrived at the Comfort Inn where we discovered that our rooms were paid for by Chad Spencer, a Freedom Writer teacher. We unpacked, did some homework, and eventually headed out to dinner with Chad. We enjoyed a wonderful dinner at a local Italian restaurant and headed back to the hotel to get to bed early. (Well, that is what we told Mr. and Mrs. Schober, we actually stayed up pretty late!) Tomorrow is the beginning of our "Be the Change" trip!

P.S. Mrs. Schober left her cell phone at Rita's next to the hotel... not a good way to start the trip!

April 15, 2011 11:17 AM

We just left West Virginia after sharing our stories with a group of 35 teachers and it was TERRIFIC! They learned a lot about each other, things they never knew before, and in the process learned about us! They were great to talk to and they showed strong emotion towards us. They did not want us to stop talking! Chad Spencer, another Freedom Writer teacher, asked us to talk to this group of teachers because they are close to being taken over by the government because of low test scores. He wanted us to teach them how important it is to get to know your students, because if you don't know matter what you say or do the learning will not happen. After 3 ½ hours of activities, discussions, the Line Game and the Toast for Change, the teachers hugged us good-bye with a promise that they will get to know their students beginning on Monday! We fulfilled our goal and we are day two into "Changing the World".

April 15, 2011 11:00 PM

After a great beginning to the day, we boarded the van and U-Haul at 10:57 AM and traveled for 10 hours until we reached Nashville. The trip was uneventful until we got within five miles of Nashville when a strong storm hit and Mrs. Schober couldn't see out the windshield. So, after a few minutes delay while we waited for the storm to pass, we finally arrived at our rental house, which is AWESOME! We unpacked, ordered some pizza from Papa John's, watched a movie, and went to bed! Tomorrow we get to meet the teachers and see Kirkpatrick for the first time! We are making some great memories! This was a great first day for what we know will be a great week!

April 16, 2011   8:24 PM

SCOOOOO! We just got back from Kirkpatrick and it was an amazing day! No words can describe today. We arrived at the school about 9:00 in the morning and everyone was so welcoming. We got a two-day task done in one day and everyone was so happy we were here! We painted the entire upstairs of the school, unloaded all the supplies and put them in the gym so we could sort them and store them, cleaned out and painted the teacher's lounge, bought a microwave, refrigerator, coffee machine, sofa, chairs, and snacks for the lounge, started to design the school mural and so much more. We didn't take too many breaks because we were so excited to be here. We met some of the students, who shared their dancing skills with us, and they were mad cool! Ms. Boone, the gym teacher, is crazy! After a long day of work, we ordered pizza, again, and realized we had a lot left over so some of the teachers asked if we wanted to deliver them to the projects where the students live. We took four pizzas over and it was sad to see where the kids are living. But one thing we all noticed was how grateful everyone was and how excited the kids were to meet us. It put a lot of things into perspective for us. We knew that we were making a difference already!

April 17, 2011   9:15 PM

Today we finished the painting, the mural, the teacher's lounge, and organizing at Kirkpatrick and then we began to clean out the playground. It was littered with so much trash and glass! We actually picked up almost 100 pounds of glass today! It is a shame to see what the kids have to deal with. It is crazy to think that little four and five year olds are running around a playground with so much glass and litter all over! The school had a cook-out for us and we ate so much! They cooked hamburgers, hot dogs and some good old fashioned Tennessee barbeque. It was bangin'!

The staff are treating us like royalty and we did not expect that. That was really nice of them, but the best part was when we went back to the projects to deliver food that we did not eat... the smiles on the children's faces cannot be described.

April 18, 2011   9:37 AM
We just woke up from a great night out on the town of Nashville! We went to the Wild Horse Saloon and had so much fun! There were so many people walking the downtown area that it took us a while to find a place to eat. We walked into the saloon and there were horses hanging upside down from the ceiling! And, there was a huge area for line dancing and... we learned a lot of country line dances! It was so much fun! We danced a lot and ate some great food. It felt good having some down time and relaxing with each other after three days of hard work. We also got to sleep in since Kirkpatrick had another day of state testing and we couldn't show up until after 11. It really felt good to relax but we need to get moving... we still have lots to do!

April 18, 2011   8:53 PM
When we arrived at Kirkpatrick, we walked into the gym and all the kids attacked us with hugs and a hundred and one questions! We didn't have to introduce ourselves because the kids knew who we were by our video we sent them! (And, since Rosa was the only girl, it was easy for her!) We then went to the cafeteria and some of the teachers were there with their students and they started yelling "SCOOO" "SCOOO" and it was hysterical! (SCOOO is our "Mix Call")

It got so crazy in the cafeteria that a couple of the kids got into a fight... that wasn't fun! We got to hang out with the kids today and really had a blast. We played with the kids outside and then we had to do some work. We started to clear out the playground area and got rid of the old equipment that we couldn't refurbish and painted the equipment that was in good condition! The one thing we all noticed was there was not one student anywhere that was not smiling! It felt magical. I don't think we could ever imagine a more perfect day!

April 19, 2011   10:50 PM

MADD WORK! Crazy tired! We don't even want to talk about today not to mention a second degree sunburn! We moved over 27,000 pounds of mulch that took us almost six hours since we only had four wheelbarrows and ten people! We also had to dig the 25 plus holes that are 18 inches deep for the playground posts, and we are EXHAUSTED! This was the first day, of course, that was hot and sunny and it was the day of the most work. Almost 10 hours of intense work! We were invited over to Dr. Stengel's house for dinner, Mrs. Schober knows her from Lancaster and she is a professor at Vanderbilt, and it was really good, but we were so exhausted we did not feel we were good company. It was a REALLY LONG DAY and we accomplished more than we ever thought possible for one day. But, tonight there are supposed to be bad storms and it is supposed to rain tomorrow when the playground is being installed. We are going to bed saying lots of prayers that everything goes as planned. It can't rain... we have done so much hard work and nothing can mess this up! We have only one more day in Nashville and we have to finish the playground...! Mrs. Schober even sent an email to all the staff and faculty back at school asking them to pray for no rain! This is too important to let a little bit of rain get in the way of making a dream come true for some great kids at Kirkpatrick!

April 20, 2011   8:00 PM

AMAZING but STRESSFUL day! We finished the playground and it didn't take that long to do! We are so happy to be done with everything we came to do but we all want to stay another day at least so we don't have to say goodbye. And, man, we all cried today! We came to school at 9:00 and there was no electricity because of the storm last night. The school had a huge assembly planned for us and they were all stressing out because nothing was going as planned. The playground was set to arrive at any minute and we knew we had to get started as soon as possible...! So, we waited and the lights finally came on and the assembly began! The whole school was there and they sang for us, read us letters, and gave us gifts... it is beyond words. There were so many tears from the kids, the teachers and all of us. It was so powerful and so full of love... it was something all of us will always remember! After the presentation, all of the MIX got up to talk and to challenge the students. We all talked and some of us shared our life stories, which was scary. Rosa even got up and talked, and she hates to talk about herself, and she cried! She was emotional because of the whole week, but she also saw a bunch of snakes and she was still a little freaked out about that! We were all proud of her! It was such an emotional day. To see the playground complete, saying good bye to all the kids and teachers, it was day that was a mix of so many crazy emotions... it was day that none of us will ever forget! We even signed each of the students T-Shirts... we felt like rock stars!!!!!!

After we said our final good-byes, we headed back to the house to clean, pack and get ready to head home. We invited some of the teachers over and we got a chance to really sit and talk with them and share our lives with each other. We all sat in a big circle and talked and talked and talked...we all got real with each other and shared stories that some of us never heard before. Through this whole trip one thing is certain... we formed a bond that will never be broken and a bond that is filled with trust and support. After everything we have done, seen and witnessed, we know there is still more to be done. This is not the last time the Mix will make a difference in the world... we plan to make a lot more kids smile! We are making a difference one step at a time!

We are proud to say our mission in Nashville is complete...!

Patrick Brennan, Ramonita Marti and "The Mix"

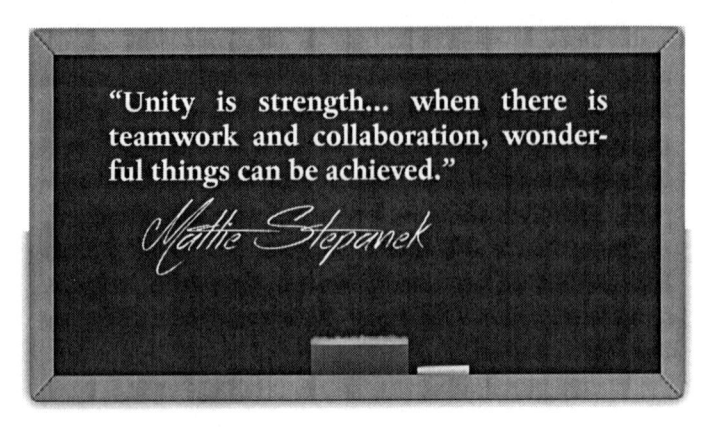

> "Unity is strength... when there is teamwork and collaboration, wonderful things can be achieved."
>
> *Mattie Stepanek*

SECRET INGREDIENT #6
Encourage Collaboration

Encouraging students to work together can be a real challenge. How do you get students to share their most intimate writing, feel comfortable when discussing different literary themes and ideas, or contemplate their inner moral voices? Working together in small groups with students that are unfamiliar to them can be a great start to understanding the different perspectives from each person. Eventually expanding to the entire class and collaborating together was reached in Room 123 time and time again and quickly became one of my favorite accomplishments.

However, sometimes the best collaboration comes not from teaching an English lesson, but rather getting involved in clubs and activities in school where the students learn firsthand the importance of working together. Seeing your students outside the classroom environment is an experience that every teacher should witness. Learning about their passions, interests and talents is a window into their souls that you may never see while in a classroom.

Notre Dame Club, Mock Trial and Kairos, a four

day spiritual retreat, were all activities that required a lot of time but allowed me to learn more about the students that walked the halls of our school. Student Council and Aevidum, however, were two activities which kept collaboration as its core requirement for success to be realized.

Student Council is a group of young people chosen by their peers to represent their class and school in a variety of venues. Between organizing Homecoming festivities, filling shoes on St. Nick Day with candy and surprises, and appearing before administration to question new rules governing the student body, the leaders had to quickly learn the importance of working, not only with each other, but also with the entire school. These are lessons that cannot be taught; they must be learned. As a moderator, I was often questioned why I did not attend certain meetings where the representatives were in attendance. The answer was simple. It was their club, their school, and they had to take ownership. They had to learn the importance of working as a team and it was my place to step back and watch the magic be created.

It was not always easy. When students would promise to do something and then not fulfill their obligation, the wrath of failure fell on the shoulders of the moderators. When an event did not go according to plan, it was the moderator who received the complaints. However, I would not change any aspect of the "learning by doing" model of which I fully believe. You learn by making mistakes. You learn by working together. You learn by understanding the importance of collaboration and communication. And that cannot be taught with notes and lectures.

We connected through working together in order to help others.

While reflecting on my time at high school and the four years I spent at Lancaster Catholic High School, there is one club, quote, and/or situation– whatever you want to call it that truly sticks out. This is that moment in your life, where everything makes sense at that point in time; everything that you went through had a point, a meaning.

Sadly, I did not have Mrs. Schober for any class. However, I was lucky enough to have her as a student council moderator. I was part of student council since my sophomore year, but specifically served my senior year on the executive council as secretary. I remember truly debating to even sign up to run for this position, because one of my friends was already on the ballot and I thought it might be one of those moments where it would not be a good idea. However, I believe that I briefly discussed it with you and Mrs. Hockley, the other moderator, and you both told me to go for it… especially when my friend decided to take her name off the ballot. Anyway, after that I was elected. The Executive Council consisted of Sean Henry, Mary Grace Reich, Maggie Larkin, and myself. Some of my favorite memories were our meetings with you discussing how we were going to improve the student council and make it a real valuable entity at LCHS again. You pushed us to work hard, accomplish what we wanted, and remind us that we were leaders. Through the work and dedication that you and Mrs. Hockley had and put forth toward Student Council, everyone on Student Council was motivated to make each event the best we could and even better than last years (Homecoming- the Dance & the entire week; Catholic Schools week; Crusader Crazy Shirts; Handbook revisions; Christmas Cards to Hannah; donation to Make a Wish for $1,200). Your door was always open for us to come to, so if we had an idea of what we wanted Student Council to work on, we knew that you were always there for us to help. Even never having had you has a teacher, I knew that I could come to you about anything or everything I might have needed help with.

As I was saying in the beginning… everything you and Mrs. Hockley taught us came to a realization when the Executive Council members went to graduation practice on Thursday and found gifts on our seats. On the wrapping paper was a note that said "Elizabeth, "Because you are!" Love and best wishes, Team Schockley". I waited until after practice and I got to my car to open it and it was a frame with a quote in it… Specifically a quote we had come across during the training of the new student council for the 2009-2010 school year. When we came across this quote, either you took it from us and said we weren't allowed to use it; even though it was one of our favorites. The quote was: "If your actions inspire others to dream more, learn more and become more, you are a leader" – John Quincy Adams. Upon opening it, I laughed (but in a good way) because I realized that you and Mrs. Hockley made us into leaders that year. You two had stolen that quote we had wanted to use during the training because you wanted to give it to us. You pushed us to lead the other members of Student Council, our class (which as you remember was not the most liked at LCHS), and to be leaders for the school. This is a lesson, which did not come without work, but it has truly been one of the most rewarding. I think that year the Executive Council, and ultimately all of Student Council, realized that what we did matter. We were not just there for a resume; we were there to make a difference; and that we COULD make a difference. You taught us that the best thing we can do for others is to set a good example for them, help them, but most importantly lead them in the right direction.

Since then, I have gone to college, where I have served as an officer for two honor societies, President and Parliamentarian for my sorority, and have been nominated *for an award that only five girls are nominated for based off of merit, scholarship, involvement, and LEADERSHIP! I also completed a semester being a student teacher and will be returning to Saint Francis in the fall for Graduate school. I will be studying Educational Leadership and will have graduate school paid for because I will have a Graduate Assistantship, where I will be helping to advise and do media for organizations under the department of student Engagement. (Such as Student Government Association, Student Actives Organization, and Greek Life) I can firmly say that none of this would have ever been possible if you (and Mrs. Hockley) had not pushed me during my time on Student Council. I learned a lot watching the example and leadership you set for me during my time in high school and even since then. I know I would not be where I am today if it were not for you. You wrote "Because you are!" but what you should have written was "We taught you well."*

Elizabeth (EB) Anastasio, Student

Aevidum is a made-up word that means "I got your back". It was started by a group of local high school students from Cocalico High School who lost one of their classmates to suicide. They felt lost and hopeless and did not want to see this happen to anyone else so they created this club that has since spread to many schools in Lancaster County. At Lancaster Catholic, the students began this club under the guise of being there for any student who needed a shoulder to lean on while also spreading awareness of the signs of teenage depression and suicide. The student leaders organized and ran every single meeting. To see them work together under one cause was magical. I was honored to be a mentor to these teens who really wanted to make a difference in the lives of their peers and spread awareness throughout the school.

The first year in its existence, the club hosted more than 150 members; the kids couldn't wait to get involved. The student officers arranged several assemblies throughout the year hosting several impactful speakers, including a father who lost his son to suicide when he was only twelve years old. His son had been a victim of cyber-bullying. You could hear the words "I got your back!" sung loudly and emphatically throughout the hallways for days after the presentation. But no assembly was as powerful as the one where a young lady stood up to tell her story in front of the student body.

On this particular day, students were taken from their classes to represent the number of teens lost due to suicide on a daily basis. For the rest of the day, the "dead" students could not speak, smile, or participate in class. At the end of the day, the entire school assembled in the gym and one-by-one the "dead" students marched in as their obituaries were being read. It was powerful. And then, a young lady stepped up to the microphone and told her story. She had contemplated suicide and wanted to share her story with others. What she said changed the lives of every person present.

We connected through pain in order to give hope.

☆ ☆ ☆

"God grants the heaviest burdens to those who can carry them." Up until four years ago, this quote did not have any special meaning to me. Today, everyone who surrounds me knows I not only have this tattooed on my ribs but it has also become a set of words I think about every single day.

Four years ago I was a college freshman who had everything I had ever wanted. I was a student-athlete at Randolph Macon College where I started and played every single soccer game throughout my rookie season. I was surrounded by parents and a sister who supported me and would do anything to make me happy. I had a boyfriend who at the time I thought was the love of my life and his family became a second family who supported me just as much as my own. For two years she was so much more than just my teacher and boyfriend's mom, she was a huge part of my life and the ups and downs. From the outside it appeared I had the perfect life and for a few months I did until three men took all of that away.

Fall break that year had started off a little different for me than most college students. Since I was an athlete we were not allowed to go home because we still had practice and a game even though we did not have any classes for a few days. Friday I went to my classes and then to practice just like a normal day. After practice I went to eat with my teammates and then I had to meet with a professor over what I had missed in class due to a game a few days prior. I will always wonder if maybe I had taken longer to eat or had walked back a different path if maybe my day would have had ended without so much pain.

On my way back to my dorm I had my name called from the men behind me. I figured it was another Lindsey since I did not recognize their voices. They called it out again and before I knew it I was surrounded by three men I did not know. To a bystander it looked like three men who *were flirting with a girl, which was normal on a college campus. We came upon one of the dorm buildings and I was pushed into the entrance. As soon as we were in the building their demeanors changed from smiling, sweet men to men who drug me by my legs and kicked me in the ribs repeatedly until I was drug into a room and the door was shut.*

For the next hour and a half it seemed that I was never going to make it out of that room, ever. I told myself that if I was dead it would be better then what they were doing. Once I was drug into the room each of them took a turn punching or kicking or whatever they wanted to me in the center of the room until I could no longer stand on my feet. If that was all they had done I believe I would not have struggled as much the following months, but that was not enough for them. Following that they each took a turn raping me while one of them sat at the desk and filmed it on their phones. I tried to focus on the wood panels on the bed above me and not what they were doing to me. The last man to go told me he would stop when I stopped crying and then laughed when I began to cry more. When they had each finished and were content with how it had gone, the tallest pushed me up against the wall and said if I ever told anyone no one would believe me and they would do it all over again. I had to promise I would never tell before they let me go. He handed me my soccer bag and told me to have a good night as he shut the door behind me.

The next twenty-four hours were the hardest of my entire life. I ran back to my dorm as quickly as my body would let me and then sat in the shower until I could no longer take the heat on my skin. No matter how hard I scrubbed, I could not get the feeling of their hands off of me. That night I sat in the laundry room crying and told my boyfriend some boys had messed with me and I left it at that. I knew as soon as I told him what had happened it would change our relationship. The next day we played Washington and Lee and, to this day, I don't know how I got through that game. That night I had to go to homecoming with my boyfriend and it took an entire bottle of makeup to cover the bruises that I had. All night I worried someone would be able to tell just by looking at me what had occurred the night before.

From that day on I fell apart in every aspect of my life but soccer. I did not go to class or go out on the weekends with friends. I secluded myself to my room and only came out to go to practice or games. I began to lose weight and show all of the other signs of depression. I even thought of killing of myself several different times. My family and friends thought I was homesick and having a difficult time adapting to college. I knew that there was no way I could survive the next four years at Macon and transferred to Elizabethtown College so I could be close to home.

Even after I had transferred I struggled to be happy and complete day-to-day tasks as simple as getting out of bed or attending classes. For months I kept what had happened to myself until my boyfriend broke up with me and then I knew I had to tell him what had been going on and why I was not myself. I will never forget the look on his face when I choked the words out "I was raped". It took me a long time to tell him the whole truth, as well as everyone else in my life. To this day no one will ever fully know what happened in that room because it is so hard for me to even wrap my head around.

After transferring, things began to get better for a while and then they all came crashing down in the fall of my sophomore year. At this point I had told my family and many people who surrounded me. I became very sick and was diagnosed with Epilepsy. The day after I came out of the hospital, my boyfriend of almost two years broke up with me and I thought I would never be ok or happy without him. I didn't think I could handle a broken heart and everything else I was going through. For so long I depended on him and his family to get me through the rape and that's all our lives became. It took me years to realize how unfair that was to not only them, but me. I will always love each of them and I will never be able to say thank you enough because I would not be here if it was not for them.

A few months later, I spoke at my high school in front of the seniors and shared my personal story. Mrs. Schober agreed that it was something seniors need to know and realize that it can happen to anyone. That was the first time my sister heard many of the details that had occurred and it broke my heart to see how much it affected her. I tried to reiterate to them that less than two years before I was the one sitting in their seat and I could have never imagined that something so terrible would have happened to me. Being able to share my story with each of them gave me a little bit of hope that things would be ok. A few weeks after that, I spoke in front of the entire student body and faculty members during an Aevidum assembly. I never imagined that I would be standing in front of my friends, teachers, parents and so many other people I loved and would be sharing a story that had the whole gym in tears. It is hard to put into words how incredible it was when my high school and the Lancaster Catholic community came together and gave me so much hope and love to push forward.

Mrs. Schober held many different roles in my life. She was not only one of my favorite teachers in high school or my boyfriend's mom, but she was someone that I knew I could come to about anything and she would help me get through it. I can honestly say that for a long time she was the one who helped me get through the after math of the rape and everything that went along with that. You may think that four years later everything is ok and I am back to who I am before I was raped. I have accepted that I will never be that person again and that's ok because life goes on. I don't think I will ever be able to understand why I was gang raped but I do know that it has made my family unbelievably strong. From the beginning of the past four years my mom always told me to remember that no matter what happens, this is always hope.

Lindsey Nester, Student

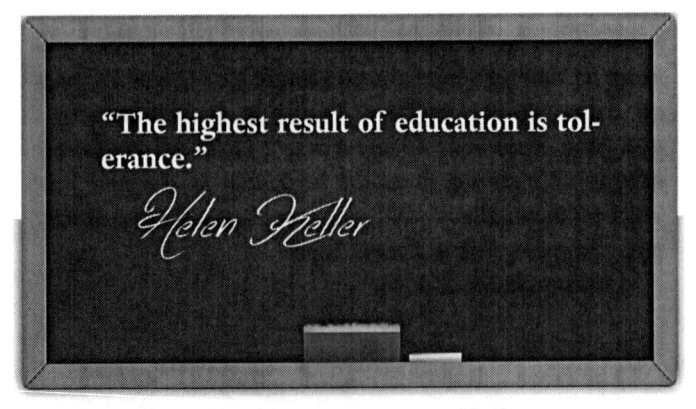

> "The highest result of education is tolerance."
> *Helen Keller*

SECRET INGREDIENT #7
Teach Tolerance

"You are so rude." "I cannot stand the way he is so loud all the time." "Why is she always the center of drama and attention?" "He is so gay." Teaching students of any age to accept others for who they are, to be open-minded, to be non-judgmental, is a hard task. When studying the Holocaust, the Rwandan Genocide, and even *Catcher in the Rye*, the idea of tolerance can be easily intertwined within the discussion and these lessons can be powerful and make students question themselves to the very core.

One such occasion happened very early in the school year. *Night,* by Eli Weisel, is a dramatic, powerful, heart wrenching memoir about one man's torture and ultimate survival during the Holocaust. But, how can you get students to understand how something horrific actually happened? The Holocaust was not always discussed in History classes, and many of my students had never been exposed to the realities of this atrocity. How was I going to bring the Holocaust to life and help them to understand that history can, and will, repeat itself? It was as easy as playing a game!

The name of the game? The Lifeboat game. I placed the students into pairs and handed them a piece of paper with directions written at the top stating that out of the fifteen people listed, only eight could be saved from demise due to their boat sinking. The life boat could only hold eight people and, as the captains, they had to choose who would survive and who would die based on the descriptions given. For example, there was a prostitute with no parents who was an excellent nurse and had already saved a drowning child. She was 37. A male criminal who was charged with murder but was the only one capable of navigating the life boat. He was 35. A crippled boy, eight years old, who had to be helped to do all the basic necessities in order to survive. After the pair decided on their list, I grouped them into fours, then eights, until the room was divided in half and they had to arrive on a group consensus. Each side is then given two minutes to state who they believe should survive and the class comes up with the final list. What they did not realize was that during their discussions, I had walked around the room and written down different phrases I heard them saying. After the final decision had been made, I started reading from the list. "Kill the prostitute." "Get rid of the retard, he won't be of any use to anyone." "Get rid of the fat guy, he will just weigh the boat down and steal what little food we have." And the list continued. The hush that overcame the room was powerful. What they were hearing were words that came from their own mouths and they were ashamed, embarrassed, and angry. I then proceeded.

"What you just did was exactly what happened during the Holocaust. Hitler decided who would live and who would die based on his own thoughts, his own ideals and his own reasoning. What just happened with our "game" was a wake-up call to all of us. That quickly, this group of loving, supportive and passionate students decided between life and death based on nothing but who that person was and what they could or could not do. That is why it is important to study the Holocaust because if we do not become more tolerant, if we do not step in when something bad is happening, the Holocaust can, and will, happen again."

Silence.

We connected through a game that opened our eyes and our minds.

✶   ✶   ✶

I remember that it was one of the first weeks of school and I came to class as I come to every class; excited with a huge side of looming pessimism (I always expected classes to be exciting, however they seldom fit that category for me). I remember that you gave us a list of people and their potential contribution to society such as a researcher looking for a cure for cancer all the way down to someone with a minimal contribution to society. You gave us the paper and told us we could choose only a certain fraction of all of them to save and asked us to come up with which people (depending on their contributions) we would save. I have a very cold logical mind when it comes to such things, so I sifted through the descriptions with ease selecting whose life to spare and whose to extinguish.

After we were finished with the exercise you asked us who we chose and we had a discussion on why we chose who we did. Proceeding the talk about who we selected you pointed out that we all chose who to live and die with ease. We decided to play God and decide who lives and dies so easily without ever thinking of refusing to do such a thing. It was then that you made the comparison of Hitler sending Jews, the mentally ill, and homosexuals to the concentration camps playing God on who dies that week. This immediately pierced through my conscience as an unacceptable leap (aka it really ruffled my tail feathers). I was quick to point out to you that I do not enjoy being compared to Hitler especially when it was just a paper assignment in class as compared to mass genocide. However, I come from a half Italian family and spent my life since 8th grade listening to aggressive hardcore metal so it probably came out less elegant and more aggressive. Then, I do not recall so clearly but I'm sure we broke off into some philosophical discussion about how the exercise was or was not an adequate comparison to Hitler playing God.

Now, something I would also like to add, something that I should have said to you at the time, however something I did not express at the time because I did not know how best to articulate my meaning. I remember later on in my high school career I came to talk to you and we reminisced on that day. You made some statement like "Oh you must have started off hating me because of that exercise". Fortunately, it was the complete opposite not because of the exercise but because of: 1. I viewed you that day as an open-minded individual which, for me, is more valuable than all the riches on earth and 2. You listened to me and questioned my beliefs. I then, and still now, never want to feel comfortable about what I believe. I always want my views questioned and to have my arguments picked apart, it makes for better stronger arguments in the future.

Finally, you listened... you might not know how valuable that is, like most never will, but for me being the youngest in a very opinionated family and always questioning the Catholic churches beliefs while attending a Catholic school. You were one of the only people that didn't immediately dismiss me as that stupid punk, or that blasphemous immature petulance. I thank you for that. You have a great head on your shoulders. Never lose that head.

Johnston Kelso, Student

In Mrs. Schober's class I learned an extremely valuable lesson that I can honestly say I use every day of my life. It has nothing to do with verbs, punctuation, or transitions between paragraphs, but rather it is about people, and knowing that each one of us, as you would say, has our own story. I'll never forget the day in class when we did "if you really knew me". While that day was "memorable" for a reason unrelated to class, what I learned IN class that day has certainly stuck with me forever.

That day I heard the stories of kids that I previously thought were your stereotypical private school students. But I learned how each of us face different challenges, and most of these people have overcome obstacles far worse than anything I could ever imagine in my own family, as dysfunctional as it can sometimes seem. But despite these differences, we all have one thing in common: we are all just people trying to make it and be happy in our own lives. Before, it was very easy for me to look at the black kid with poor grades and assume he was some stupid thug that didn't care about his classes. Boy was I wrong.

Before experiencing your class, it never occurred to me that maybe the reason he has poor grades was because he doesn't have time for homework because he has to make dinner for himself and his three siblings because his father is not around and his mother is addicted to crack. I believe this is called empathy. Having the opportunity to spend time in room 123 has definitely changed my life for the better.

I truly do apply this single lesson in life every day. It does not take much time for me to hear one of my friends make generalizations about people, the same generalizations I used to make, that are extremely and totally 100% naive and completely off base and uneducated. In your class I have learned that each of us has a story, and before we start talking about people, we first must listen to what it is they have to say.

Adam Law, Student

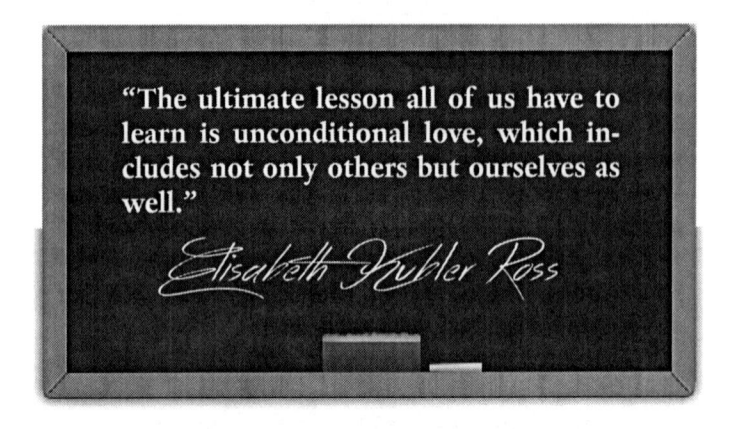

> "The ultimate lesson all of us have to learn is unconditional love, which includes not only others but ourselves as well."
>
> *Elisabeth Kubler Ross*

SECRET INGREDIENT #8
Promote Diversity

Learning about my students was always at the forefront of my curriculum which allowed me to embrace the WHOLE student, not just the "English" student sitting in front of me. Through writing, discussions, literature and one-on-one talks, I learned a lot about their backgrounds, stresses, hopes and dreams. But, how did I get them to understand that beyond the walls of our school there were many other people who had stories, heartbreaks and successes that needed to be heard in order to fully appreciate their lives and the world around them? I took them out into the world!

Nashville was our first step, and it was more successful than any of us could have imagined, but it was also important for my students to look at their own community; the people who made up our own little world. Through my Communication classes, the students were able to create a project that they wanted to work on for the year. Many ideas always surrounded their thoughts including working with animals, Habitat for Humanity and many, many others. One year, the class settled on working for a local orphanage and their eyes were opened to a world where heartache and hopefulness intertwined together to create a magical home for needy children.

Our first visit consisted of meeting with the director of the home and wrapping all the Christmas gifts for the children. There were piles and piles of donated gifts that took twenty of us almost four hours to complete. As we wrapped the gifts, my students learned the history of the orphanage as well as the stories of the kids and how they came to be at the orphanage. Some were taken away because of drug addicted parents, others were placed because of abuse or neglect, and we learned that for one young boy this home was his forty-second shelter. In my class, I had students from all economic backgrounds, ethnicities and family dynamics, but seeing the world through a child's life who had no permanent home was powerful and helped them to appreciate what they do have instead of want they didn't. They visited the orphanage once a month and loved playing with kids, bringing them gifts and cooking dinner for them and the house parents. Whether they made macaroni and cheese, chicken nuggets, tacos or spaghetti, the children were gracious and enjoyed spending time with my students. Each time we left, a piece of our hearts remained with them.

The following year, the Communications class was given a slightly different task. They were asked to discover a problem in their community and then to create a solution. What I thought was going to be a difficult task instead became a powerfully life-altering assignment for my students.

In my class was a beautiful young lady who lived

in the inner city with a single mother, several brothers and a sister. Her father had been in jail from when she was a little girl. Another student in the class lived in an affluent neighborhood, both parents at home, and successful siblings. Her life was the complete opposite. This scenario played over and over in my class and yet I challenged them to reach a consensus of what their project would be for the year.

Each student discovered a problem and created a solution to the problem and shared their idea to the class through a power point presentation followed by a question and answer session. The first young lady stood up to give her presentation and there was not a dry eye in the class.

"This past summer," she began, "I was kicked out of my house. My mom has a new boyfriend and we do not get along at all. Yea, I have a big mouth and all, but I don't deserve the disrespect that I have been getting. I do all the cleaning, all the cooking, I take care of my brother and sister. I don't know what else she wants from me? One night we got into a big argument and she kicked me out. I had nowhere to go. After a few nights on the street, I called my friend and she let me spend the night with her. For the next two weeks, I couch surfed until my mom called and told me I could come home."

The class was silent. Her story was powerful and they wanted to know more. She continued.

"While I was on the streets, I realized how lucky I was because I had a friend I could stay with. But, what about those kids who don't have anywhere to go? Who don't have friends they can count on? Who don't have family they can turn to? Where do they go? Nowhere. They stay on the streets. We need to fix this. Lancaster needs a place for teens to go to when they have been kicked out or have run away from home. We need to build a place for these kids to go and we can call it Building Hope."

It didn't matter where they came from or where they lived, my students connected with the reality that in our city were homeless teens who had nowhere to go and they wanted to help. After all the presentations were given, the class decided they wanted to create a homeless shelter for teens. They immediately got to work.

The class created a group name for themselves, much like the Freedom Writers, and called themselves "Together as One". They developed a business proposal, created power point presentations, presented to the mayor and County Commissioners, had numerous articles written about them, and even had their story and vision in a magazine. They wanted to create a safe place for teens, which was run by teens, but no one was willing to help. There was no money to be found and the students were feeling defeated. And then, in December, they received a phone call.

After months of dead ends, a church finally agreed to house Building Hope. While it was not going to be an overnight shelter, it was a beginning and the kids were ecstatic.

The first few weeks there was very little turnout. They had prepared a hot meal, bought toothbrushes, toothpaste, socks, blankets, deodorant and fruit to give to any teen who was in need of help, but no one showed up. During those weeks we sat as a class, shared our stories, bonded, and waited. And then, our first teen walked through the door. The joy that exuded from my student's faces was priceless. They were scared, excited, nervous, and happy all mixed together! And then, **it** happened.

Week after week, more and more teens walked through the doors. They met with the teens, learned of their stories, offered them food, counsel, and support. The lives of the teens who came into Building Hope were unbelievably sad, heartbreaking and triumphant. Some were bullied, many were dealing with abuse, physical, sexual and mental, some contemplated suicide, and others were cutters. My students listened, cried, guided and helped these teens get through another week.

"Together as One", the students learned about the diverse world in which they live because of Building Hope, a safe haven for teens. They heard some horrific stories and witnessed the transformation that can happen when one person takes the time to listen, understand, and care about a complete stranger. They learned about life.

We connected by understanding and accepting diversity.

Imagine having somewhere to go just to talk to someone for a few hours and have no one judge you. Everyone has a story, you just have to be willing to listen. That is what Building Hope is all about. A judgment free zone where someone you never thought would go through the same thing you are is dealing with the same problems.

Junior year is one of the most important years of high school. Walking in the first day of school, going to all of your classes, having the same old classes' just new teachers and harder material. But one class made that regular routine change. Communications was hands on learning. The class picked a project and that's what you worked on for the year. My class volunteered at Christ's Home for Children, and wrote and published a book.

Fast forward one year; senior year. Starting out senior year I was in another hands on learning class called Senior Seminar. It was very similar to Communications but you had the last two periods of the day to work instead of only having one. We could also leave the school if we needed to. My partner and I started our project which was starting a runaway safe haven for teenage girls. The Communications class was also doing a project that was basically the same thing, only they wanted to open a runaway shelter for boys and girls. Grouping together with them we became **Together as One: Building Hope.** *There were so many different things to accomplish in so little time, but we were ready for the commitment. We presented to many different organizations and churches. They all loved our idea but couldn't help as much as they would have liked to. After thirteen "No's", on December 11, 2012, we received the voicemail that we had been waiting for. St John's Episcopal Church would allow us to use their space. February 19, 2013, was the opening date for Building Hope and everyone was excited to see what was in store for us.*

After handing out countless flyers and getting the word

out, our third week of being "open" we had our first two guests. We were all so excited to see that this was actually becoming a reality and it was just starting to grow. Since our opening date, we have had roughly 25 different kids come through and tell us a little bit of their stories.

Building Hope is something that is so much different from any other organization. When you walk into the meeting place it is a judgment free zone. It is a place for you to get away, if only for a few hours because it isn't an overnight thing... yet. But, the experience that you have there is something that I couldn't express on paper. Complete strangers come in and trust you with things they might not even tell their best friends. But the best part of it all is we get to help them through their problems. The advice that has been handed out at the meetings every week has been life changing, not only to myself but for everyone who gets to witness it firsthand. Building Hope, for me, has been a life changing experience. It was something we created, starting from nothing except a classroom with an idea. It has been a place that I can get away from all my worries and anything that is going on in my life and help someone else with their struggles. The process to get us this far hasn't been an easy one, but I wouldn't change one thing about it. Every different face and story makes us able to help someone new that comes in the door. It is a place run by teens for teens. For me this is what I want to do for the rest of my life. Help other people through their rough times.

Bridgette Barrett, Student

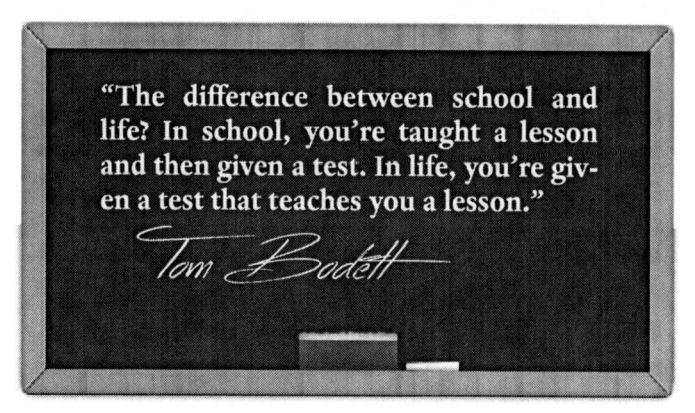

> "The difference between school and life? In school, you're taught a lesson and then given a test. In life, you're given a test that teaches you a lesson."
>
> *Tom Bodett*

SECRET INGREDIENT #9
Create Community

Telling my dad about my rape was one of the hardest things I ever had to do. It happened so long ago. I never told him. Instead, I drank myself sick, literally, and still I never told him. I just couldn't bear to see the look on his face. He was the one man who wanted nothing more than to protect me, and I neglected him that responsibility. Looking back on those days, and the many that followed, I could have told him on numerous occasions, but I never did. It all came down to one day, one moment. My dad, myself, and my students. Together we were going to tell my dad about that horrible and life-changing event that occurred when I was eighteen.

How did I finally get to this point and why my classroom? Why would my students be present in such a private and emotional personal moment? Because I needed them and I knew my father would, as well.

Two years after becoming a Freedom Writer Teacher, Erin Gruwell organized a reunion of all the teachers from across the United States and Canada.

It was powerful seeing all those inspirational teachers in one room, and being a part of them was overwhelming. It was four days of pure magic ending with an unbelievable announcement: We were going to write a book! One of my dreams was to be a published author, and that dream was coming true beyond my wildest imagination. All 150 of us were going to be a part of book called *Teaching Hope* and each of us were to write one story/entry, mimicking the Freedom Writers Diary format. We would each be anonymous; no one would know our story unless we wanted to publicly acknowledge our entry. By doing this, we had freedom to write about our most personal experiences as classroom teachers. We were safe.

I immediately penned my first entry to have the Foundation peruse. I used an extended metaphor throughout the entire piece, reflecting on one day in the life of my classroom using a roller coaster as my continuous symbol. I thought it was perfect! I sent it away with butterfly's in my stomach… I could not wait to hear praises and accolades from the Foundation! Only a few days had passed and I received the phone call I was waiting so impatiently for. Sue Ellen, an original Freedom Writer student, was on the other end.

"Hi Anne. It's Sue Ellen."

"Hi Sue Ellen! So, what did you think of my piece for the book?"

The next words that came from her soft-spoken soul were not what I was expecting.

"Anne, anyone could have written that! You know what you have to write about!"

"What?? That piece was so me! Nobody else could have written that! That was a day in the life of

MY classroom. Nobody else's!"

"Anne, listen to me. I know it is going to be hard. Believe me, I know, but you need to write about your rape."

My heart sank. Sue Ellen was right. What happened to me in college was still haunting me and I needed to write about it.

"Okay. I will do it. But it won't be easy."

"I know you can do it. And if you need me for anything, just remember I am a phone call away."

I hung up the phone and my whole body was shaking. How was I going to take so many emotions, thoughts, and pain and transcribe that one event onto paper? I grabbed my computer and allowed my stream of consciousness to overcome my hands as I slowly composed my story. What transpired was overwhelming. I had sheltered those thoughts for so long that when I saw them in print it made me realize that I could finally begin to heal and hopefully help others, as well.

Writing about my rape was difficult, but nothing compared to telling my father. I knew that in August of 2009, *Teaching Hope* would be published and I would go on book signings and maybe even read my entry publicly. Yet, my father had no idea which entry was mine. He was so proud of me! He told everyone he met, knew, and didn't know that his daughter was a published author! And yet, he had no idea.

My father was always been the one person I could count on to tell me what I needed to hear, not what I wanted to hear. He was the one person I looked to as a role model, an inspiration, a guide that lead with a soft heart and disciplined soul. I knew he would be perfect for a group of my students that needed a strong role model in their life. And so I asked my dad to come into my classroom once a week and mentor The Mix. And, without hesitation, my dad jumped on board. He came in and talked about worldly topics, politics, life and so much more. The kids would meet him at the door and escort him to room 123, proudly smiling and grinning from ear to ear. They loved "Mr. P" and all that he stood for. My dad became a huge part of their lives which is why I knew that I needed to show my father my *Teaching Hope* entry in Room 123. A place where we both felt safe, secure and loved. A place where family met every day.

I picked a day that I had an hour long block of time and I waited patiently as the kids met my dad at the entrance to the school and walked him to our classroom. As he entered, my heart was breaking. I knew I was about to tell him something that would tear him apart. As my father entered, we did something out of the ordinary. The Mix, myself, and my dad all stood in a circle and held hands. Then, two of my students, Patrick and RJ, began a prayer asking for patience, healing and love. My dad looked confused and worried. We then took our seats and I shakily began my practiced speech:

"Dad, today is going to be a little different. Today is a day that I never wanted to come, but I have no choice anymore. As you know, I have co-authored *Teaching Hope* and my entry is not signed. We are all anonymous, yet I want you to know which one is mine."

I took my father by his hand and led him to my desk where my story was waiting. Before he started to read, he looked at me with worried eyes and said, "Please tell me you do not have cancer."

"I promise, Dad, I don't have cancer."

With silence, he tilted his head down and began

to read. I could see his shoulders tense. I witnessed a transformation of my stoic and strong father into a person who looked lost and heartbroken. He looked up at me and, with sadness and tears in his eyes, he said, "Why didn't you tell me?"

"I couldn't", I struggled to say.

"No", he said, "you wouldn't."

Suddenly the class bell rang and the kids, slowly and cautiously, came up to my father and gave him hugs as each of them cried. They then hugged me tightly and said "I love you" as they headed out the door. It was now the two of us.

I didn't know what to do next. But, as always, my father knew exactly what to do. He held me. He held me so long I didn't want him to let go. We cried together as we both grieved and accepted what happened to me when I was eighteen years old. Suddenly a knock on the door broke our sacred moment.

My principal came by to see if I was okay, the same person who questioned why I spoke about my rape in my classroom a few years prior. I had told him what I was going to do that morning, and he wanted to check on my father. I watched as the two men talked about what had happened just moments before. I don't remember much about that conversation, but I do remember that it helped to have him there for support, for both of us. When my principal left, I knew I had to walk my dad out to his car before my next class came in, but I wasn't ready for him to leave. I felt there was so much more to say. I turned to my dad, shaking, and started to cry. He held me so tightly. I felt safe. I felt warm. I felt free.

He broke free from our embrace, and staring directly into my eyes he said, "I have always loved you and I have always been proud of you. But I had no idea how strong of a person you really were until today. I admire you for so many reasons, but I admire you mostly for being the person you are today and all that you have been through. You suffered on your own. You survived on your own. You are stronger than I ever thought. I love you, Dawd." With those words, he gently kissed me on my forehead, and we walked out of my classroom hand-in-hand into our newfound respect for each other.

We connected through the power of love.

Over 25 years ago, a date-rape occurred at a college in Erie, PA. The female victim was a student at Gannon University. It was not reported to University or other campus officials. I don't know why. Did she feel she was partially at fault, limiting the "perps" responsibility? Did she feel guilt, too? Was she too high on something put in her drink? Or did she just have too much alcohol, period? All I know that female student is my younger daughter/middle child and I found out about the attack roughly three years ago when she showed me the section in a book she was co-authoring. And now she wants me to write a commentary in her book. What do I say? Why didn't she tell me about this a long time ago? Did she tell her mother who has since died? Did her mother keep it from me? That I will never know. But now that I do know, what do I say? That is the easy part. I love her so very much and am extremely proud of her many accomplishments... as a spouse, mother, teacher, student counselor, among many other achievements. Above all, she is a very loving and caring person and she is my Dawd. I just wish I had known about this before so I could have given her what she has given me all these years, a big and caring shoulder. As we say in our family, "Keep your chins", Anne.

Dennis T. Penny, Sr. – Anne's father

My father does not like to talk about what happened to me. I can only imagine the way he feels; not being able to protect his daughter, the secrets, the hidden words. And, when I asked him to write about that morning when he learned of my rape, he was hesitant and did not want to "go back in time" to a moment that he could not control. So, while his words may seem distant, it is his reality. He does not want to remember, and I cannot blame him for his honesty. As were emailing each about his entry for my book, he wrote the following to me:

Dawd: Very well put which, on paper, can be so painful as you are actually "looking" at your thoughts coming from your heart and soul, not just hearing them and letting the winds take them away. They are always a reminder.... staring at you, never going away. I love you and am so proud.

Dad

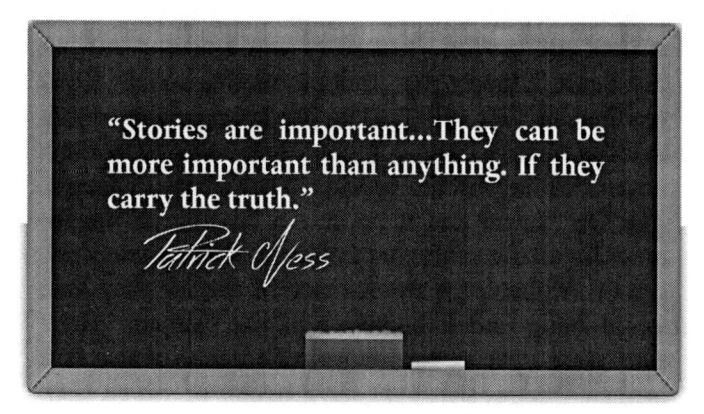

> "Stories are important...They can be more important than anything. If they carry the truth."
>
> *Patrick Ness*

Secret Ingredient #10
BUILD BRIDGES

Sometimes you have to think outside the box in order to gain the interest of your students. That does not necessarily mean dressing up as Shakespeare or jumping on your desk, although, I have enjoyed my share of desk jumping and dancing to liven things up! The hardest part about teaching Literature and writing, or any subject, was how to make it relevant for my students. How would I get them to connect to a novel that was written before they were born?

While my daughter, Michelle, was a student at Villanova University, I received a phone call from her telling me about Khaled Hosseini who was coming to her school. *The Kite Runner* was the book that the entire school read that year and the author was visiting their school. She was beyond excited. I asked her to take notes and let me know what she thought. In the meantime, I picked up a copy of the novel and started devouring each word. I turned each page with eagerness and anticipation. When she came home for fall break, she brought her pages of notes with her and told me all she learned from this remarkable author and person. His story was amazing and, in my heart, I knew my students would benefit from reading his first novel. The life lessons were many and the history behind Afghanistan was key to their understanding of the world. That spring, I taught *The Kite Runner* and it became a favorite of the seniors for all the years that followed. We watched videos on Afghanistan and learned of the life they lead while living under the ruling of the Taliban. Their eyes were opened to a world of torture, abuse and horrific images that exposed a reality of which they knew little.

Each year that followed, I added a new book based on which authors were coming to our area, so that I could give my students the chance to meet the people who had the strength to tell their stories, just like I wanted my own students to do. We read *A Long Way Gone*, by Ishmael Beah, and learned of his journeys and struggles as a child soldier. The students then went to hear him speak when he visited Millersville University. We read *Enriques Journey*, by Sonia Nazario, and they learned of her experiences as she captured the stories of those people who risked their lives to come to America for freedom. When I taught *The Things They Carried*, by Tim O'Brien, we made a trip to Washington D.C. to visit the Vietnam War Memorial and walk the treasured grounds of Arlington Cemetery. For my students to see how many people lost their lives to save their own was powerful. Through these books, the students learned of their own prejudices and it frightened them. Literature has a way of raising questions, making us think, and touching on subjects that many consider "voodoo". We discussed stereotypes, immigration laws, drug use, the Vietnam War, and more. Finding the books that tore at my student's inner core was powerful and building the bridges between the written word and reality was one of the most important lessons I ever taught.

Teaching about the Holocaust was a staple in my curriculum and bringing Holocaust survivors into my classroom was a vital component. We were blessed to have the opportunity to meet such courageous and strong people and giving my students a chance to meet a hero was the connection I needed to bring Holocaust literature to life.

I remember the first time I met a Holocaust survivor. I was in Long Beach for the Freedom Writers Institute, and was blessed to have the opportunity to meet Renee Firestone, a beautiful survivor who shared her story with Erin and her students, and gave us the opportunity to learn her story, as well. I was brought to tears as she spoke and when I saw the tattooed number on her arm, my heart was broken. From that moment on, I knew that my students needed to have the same opportunity. I did everything in my power to make sure that my students would learn firsthand about the atrocities and terror that each Holocaust victim experienced.

I contacted the local Jewish center and was immediately put in touch with a few Holocaust survivors who lived nearby. Knowing what a gift this was for my students, I needed them to take responsibility. They made welcome signs, organized lunches, and bought gifts for them to make them feel loved and welcomed. I even had kids sign up to escort them to the gymnasium. While the survivors spoke, there was silence. While my students listened, you could see tears and uncertainty surrounding their eyes.

After the presentations, every single speaker was treated like royalty. They had their pictures taken, they were surrounded by students that wanted to give them hugs, and they were treated to a lunch where the students served them. And, when we discussed the presentation in class the next day, the students were astonished at the stories told. That was something I could not teach. It was something they needed to experience. We also went to the Holocaust Museum where they walked through history and came face to face with artifacts, stories, and faces of those lost. At the end of each school year, this trip was always the one most remembered and most meaningful.

Building bridges and finding the connections was difficult and a very time consuming part of my teaching career. Putting together field trips and organizing speakers and figuring out schedules on an already tightened calendar was challenging. However, it was too important not to include. As Edmund Burke once said, "Those who don't know history are doomed to repeat it."

We connected through literature, history and life.

☆   ☆   ☆

Through various "agree/disagree" debates we had in class, I had other people question and test my thoughts and belief in a controlled setting. Not many classes have me that opportunity, and it was really good for me to have. I think the Agree/Disagree that impacted me the most was the first one where we talked about whether Hitler was evil or insane. I believed he was insane, as did four other classmates, but everyone else thought he was evil. We debated about it for a while, and while both sides had made good arguments, our opinions stayed the same. What makes this one stick out was when we were at the Holocaust museum, the other side's arguments were in my mind as I walked through. By the end of our time there, I completely switched sides. I just remember thinking "there was no way he was just insane". It just shows that sometimes discussions like that don't really affect your beliefs until you're confronted with the situation directly. I also learned a lot from reading Enrique's Journey, Night, *and* The Kite Runner. *They caused me to think about things, like immigration amnesty, which I had not previously thought of. The trip to the Holocaust Museum was incredibly powerful, and I will never forget it. Thank you for bringing literature to life and making it impactful on my thoughts, words, and actions.*

Emily Saporetti, Student

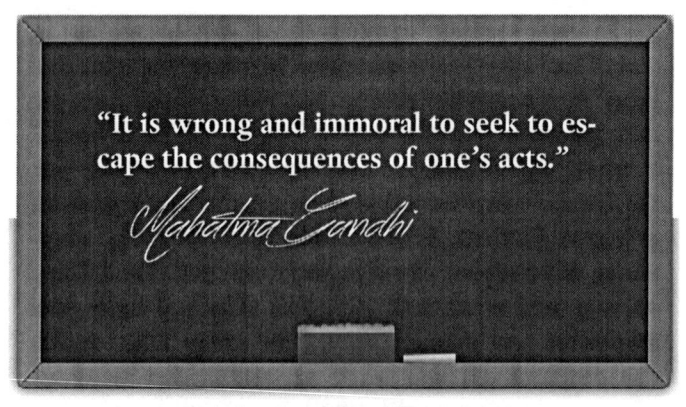

> "It is wrong and immoral to seek to escape the consequences of one's acts."
>
> *Mahatma Gandhi*

SECRET INGREDIENT #11
EXPECT ACCOUNTABILITY

Giving a test at the end of a unit, marking it for a grade, and plastering it on a report card did not make a student accountable. It simply meant they could take a test, either successfully or unsuccessfully. I despised tests. I didn't believe they really proved what a student had mastered or learned. Filling in bubbles, matching words with definitions, or regurgitating what was said in class did not mean that a student had learned much of anything. Some may argue with my thoughts on this very sensitive matter, but holding a student responsible for their own learning and making it relevant to them showed the depth of learning that the student had achieved on a deeper level.

I came to this conclusion quite early on in my teaching career. Each summer the students in my College Composition class had to read two summer novels. It was my responsibility to "test" their reading during the first week of school. I created a test which featured multiple choice, matching, true and false and a few random short answer questions. I thought it was a great way to test their knowledge as well as to see who actually read the requirements. After grading all the exams, I was pleasantly surprised. Almost all the classes had passed and there were even several perfect scores. The following week, I delved right into the novels, asking the students higher level questions which required using critical thinking skills. No one answered. I was lost. One afternoon during lunch, a few students came up to my room to chat and I asked them why no one was responding or participating in class. They looked at me in shock.

"Mrs. Schober, we hate to tell you this, but most of us never even opened the books. We haven't read a book since we came to high school!"

I was floored!

"So how did everyone pass the test?"

They laughed.

"We have learned how to take tests. Every year we get the same kind of test and each year we read Spark Notes and pass with flying colors. It is really quite simple."

One student, of whom I will keep anonymous, never read a single book but received honor status, and scored an almost perfect score on the SAT. He had learned how to take a test. Once I learned of his "talent", I turned all my tests into essay exams in which students would receive a question we had not discussed in class, find connections from the novel we were studying, and then relate it to their world and life. By the end of the year, the student who had learned how to take tests barely passed my class. I was finally holding him accountable for learning. From that moment on, I knew that my testing was going to be more relevant and require "thinking outside the box", but the students would be a big part of this process.

My goal was not to fail anyone. My goal was to teach beyond the textbook, to help them make connections, and my assessments grew from that concept. When studying the Holocaust and reading *Night*, the students had to take a theme, symbol, or idea from the book and create a multi-genre project showcasing their chosen topic through a variety of genres. When reading *The Kite Runner*, I wanted the students to explore the idea of "can you make good again?" So, I asked the students if they would be interested in completing "Random Acts of Kindness" and document what they did through writing, video, song, etc. The students were very excited. Some took it seriously, while others waited until the last minute to complete their task, but at least they did something. One student gave his new coat away to a homeless person whom he had passed by many times on the street. Another student worked at their grandparent's home who could no longer take care of their yard work. Another student wrote a letter of apology to an old friend, read it aloud in class, and professed her feelings in front of everyone. It took a lot of guts for her to make amends, and it was a powerful lesson of trying to make good again, something that was at the heart of *The Kite Runner*.

While teaching my memoir class, it was not possible to test at all. Their grades consisted of writing on a daily basis with larger projects sprinkled throughout, culminating in their own abbreviated memoir. But, I wanted them to go beyond their own stories. I wanted them to learn the importance of hearing and learning the stories of others. So, we picked up our notebooks and pens, boarded a bus, and made our way to a retirement home where each student interviewed a resident and learned their story. Prior to visiting, each student had to learn how to interview, listen, and how to take notes to capture the important moments.

When we arrived, I could see their nerves getting the best of them. We gathered in the central living area of the home, learned more about the residents, and then each student was matched with a fellow resident. I walked the halls, stood outside the rooms and eavesdropped as I heard my student's converse with ease. There was laughter, there were tears, and the memories that were being recalled were priceless. The students were overwhelmed and could not wait to start writing the stories of the older generation. They spent weeks perfecting their pieces, being careful not to disappoint their new "friend". Once they were polished, the stories were then turned into a book which the class presented to the home. They made a difference in the lives of many and, more importantly, they learned the importance of writing to record the stories that need to be heard. They learned more from that one activity than could be taught in a classroom.

I held my students accountable by creating opportunities for them to succeed while showing what they learned through their own personal connections. It was powerful and they learned more from these experiences than simply memorizing dates, names, and events.

We connected through opportunities which held them accountable for their learning about life and the possibilities that await.

I was never a good learner to begin with but I was always a very good student. I will admit that I was not always the most motivated and hardworking, and I am a very lazy person overall, and that really reflected in school. But, I always try my best and I do believe that I am naturally pretty smart (but not in science or math.) I am a pretty good student, was consistently on the honor roll in high school and on the dean's list in college, but test taking was my downfall. It really affected me because it made me feel really stupid. It was discouraging and growing up, a lot of my teachers made me feel like that was the only way to judge how smart a person was. When I took Mrs. Schober's class senior year, all of that changed. I learned that "Everybody is a genius. But if you judge a fish by its ability to climb a tree, it will live its whole life believing that it is stupid."— <u>Albert Einstein</u>. We were tested every day but not only by a stupid piece of scantron paper and a #2 pencil. We were tested by judgment, character, beliefs, behavior, thoughts, opinions, incite, everything. And I loved that because it gave those of us a chance that could not necessarily excel through testing. It gave us a chance to show what we've really got, how brilliant we really can be. I loved coming in on days when Mrs. Schober would post giant pieces of notebook paper around the classroom walls with a statement or quote and we would respond with our opinions and thoughts. Out of all of my classes that I took at Catholic, even my honors math and science courses, English class is where I felt smartest and savvy, for the first time. It was where I was able to share my deepest thoughts, strongest beliefs, and unconventional opinions either in a heated debate or in an accepting and open-minded group discussion. I learned about myself, and others, and different religions and cultures, and the things that really matter to me. I learned how to treat people, how to feel, how to react to losing a friend, how to accept others, how to get *along with someone that disliked you, how to find your passion, how to follow your dream and how to stand up for what was right, no matter what.*

I also took a speech class with Mrs. Schober, which was always one of my favorite classes to go to. I was always able to go to class and learn something without having to learn it through a boring lecture or stupid article in a giant textbook with too many words. I learned by applying and doing things myself. Instead of teaching us oral speech and then testing us on paper, she would have us do an actual speech with a different subject and goal and see if we learned anything by this. I always thought that the best way to learn and truly knowing something was by doing it yourself, which is exactly what she made us do.

In English class we would do the same. If a character in a book was going through something, we would do it, too. We would try to feel the same things they felt. One time one of our projects was an act of kindness. The project is pretty self-explanatory; you did a big or a bunch of small acts of kindness and then write about it. It was awesome and it was a really good and humbling experience. That's the stuff that I think matters the most- learning about yourself and who you really are and in Mrs. Schober's class, I found out a lot about myself and who I want to become. I consider myself successful.

Anita Carreon, Student

I'm going to be completely honest when I say that ever since I came into existence back in the late 80s, I was not an avid fan of writing. This partially stems from a long period of prepubescent life spent trying to write three sentence stories and how not to deviate from the tried and true "I wanted [object], but dad said 'no'." Evidently, I was too avaricious for my own good as a child. I also despised writing from the general standpoint that I could be acting on the things I imagine in my head, so why bother writing?

Having nurtured these beliefs in my heart--or perhaps letting them fester--I came into possession of a rather sarcastic and somewhat satirical writing style, which explains my love for Terry Pratchet and Douglas Adams, but I digress. Mrs. Schober was the first teacher I had that was actually okay with my fierce criticisms of a self-hating sort of writing. That is, I wrote to make fun of writing itself, but she let me experiment with that in class. Admittedly, to this day, I don't spend an excessive amount of time on creative writing, but I still do when it strikes my fancy and I am often coming up with ideas for writing about. I like to think my writing has taken a whimsical turn after 15 years of reading sci-fi and fantasy laced with a little bit of thermodynamics (I'm a free spirit). More often than not, I think about composing sentences in such a way as to abuse the English language without actually breaking any grammatical or usage rules. My goal is use words in unlikely ways, because, frankly: I'm not satisfied with the way things are and I feel it is my place to make it odder, if I possibly can.

Because I'm still not happy with that mess of a paragraph above, I'll sum it up as follows: Her attitude to let me write as I chose has inspired me to have fun with writing by actually making fun of writing itself. In my own way, I still despise writing, and by deprecating it, even at the cost of enjoying it, I can create my own little Ode to Hate. I

think that was one of the poems I wrote. Maybe it was Ode to Sadness? It was contradictory. I love contradictions. You have my two cents. It's been a pleasure being your student.
    Michael Anspach, Student

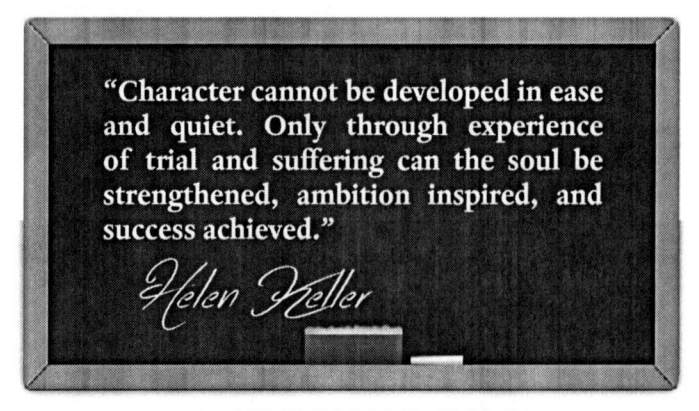

> "Character cannot be developed in ease and quiet. Only through experience of trial and suffering can the soul be strengthened, ambition inspired, and success achieved."
>
> *Helen Keller*

SECRET INGREDIENT #12
Celebrate Success

It is often said that you can say many positive statements about a person but one negative statement is what they will remember forever. How true that is in so many of life's events. As a classroom teacher, I tried to always be the bearer of positive words so that my students could feel successful and appreciated, even on their worst of days. But, in reality, many of my students were suffering from low self-esteem due to poor test grades, awkward social skills and trying to feel accepted amongst their peers.

My job was to celebrate their successes, no matter how small they may be. One of the most life-changing events I experienced while at the Freedom Writers Institute was the Toast for Change. It allowed us to put our past behind us, put the future ahead of us, and publicly proclaim what we wish to change. It was powerful because we publically exclaimed our thoughts and it allowed us to also share our failures and successes. I knew that my freshman class would benefit the most from this experience, so I set to work.

I ventured into my classroom over the weekend to prep for our Toast for Change which would happen on Monday morning. I moved all the desks to the outer walls and decorated the room with streamers and posters. In the front of the room stood a lone table filled with champagne glasses waiting to be filled with sparkling cider. My heart was racing... I knew that this celebration would bring our family together.

Monday morning came and the bell was going to ring. I quickly filled the glasses and the kids began filling the room. Their faces were priceless... questions were exuding from their eyes. I began by telling them that Erin Gruwell challenged her students to make a change, to show that they are responsible for making their own decisions and choices. I then read to them the following:

"I want you to take one of these glasses of sparkling cider, and I want each of you to make a toast. We're each going to make a toast for change. And what that means is from this moment on every voice that told you "You can't" is silenced."

Slowly each student took a glass of sparkling cider and we stood silently in a circle. I began with my toast for them and one by one they each took a turn publicly stating what they wanted to change.

"I am going to graduate from high school and go on to college. I will be the first in the family to do that."

"I am going to try to get along with my dad. I am sick of our fighting. I am tired of letting him down. I am going to try to do be a better son."

"I am going to do my homework and stop making excuses."

And then Ben began to speak.

"In the past I have been rejected by others because

of my special talents. People would torture and criticize me for all I did. But now, things have changed. I finally have a loving class of 18 who like me the way I am, along with one of my oldest friends who has been there for me since first grade. I thank you all for your help, care, and fine understanding of my needs and problems. RJ and P-Turtle – thank you for your humorous acts, they really brighten up my day. Nicolette and Stephanie, thanks for always cheering me up when I am down because of bad grades. Jazz, don't ever let anyone tell you that you are bad at art, I have learned a lot from you. Thank you all for not giving up on me."

After Ben spoke, the class became more emotional and began spilling their hearts and souls. The next hour was spent becoming a family and publically voicing their fears, wants, and challenges in order to allow success to enter their lives. That day changed our class... that day we become a real family. That day a bond was formed and lives were changed. We left with tears in our eyes and full hearts... a Toast for Change was only our beginning.

That day marked a new beginning. The kids began to trust me and each other and, because of that, we transformed our classroom into a working room. They brought in their homework during study halls. They worked on Science, Math and History together and quickly became accountable to each other. If someone did not turn in a homework assignment, they "told" on them. If someone was failing a class, we figured out TOGETHER how to help them. The change in the kids was remarkable, but it was far from perfect. I lost a few students along the way, which was heartbreaking. One student was sent to a Mental Health facility and did not come back the rest of the year. Another student did not like the private school setting, kept getting into trouble, and was eventually kicked out. Another student felt "too smart" for the class and requested to move. But, through it all, the students persevered.

We traveled to New Jersey to see Erin Gruwell speak and the kids felt like the important people I knew they were. They acted as her body guards and were very protective of her. Whenever she was on the East Coast, we raised money, rented vans, and traveled to hear her inspirational words. She called them by name and she believed in them. And, because of that, they did not want to let her down.

Four years later, they had become known to the school as The Mix. They continued to struggle with academics and personal issues, but they made it. They graduated and became the first class of Freedom Writers at Lancaster Catholic High School. They succeeded beyond my own expectations, but, more importantly, they proved to themselves that anything was possible. They learned how to set goals and achieve their dreams. They learned to believe in themselves while encouraging others along the way. They learned the power of positive thinking. And it all began with The Toast for Change.

We connected through our failures and our successes.

Walking up the steps to homeroom all I could remember hearing was Mrs. Schober saying Monday will be Toast for Change day. All I could think to myself was "what the hell does that mean?" I got into the room and there were streamers all around the room and a big table of sparkling cider and glasses. Mrs. Schober said everyone get in a big circle. People began saying things about the class and themselves. At the beginning of the year I didn't really want to do any work or listen that much and after the toast I felt like I did enough playing around; it was time to work. So I made my toast to get serious about school. I remember that day as being very emotional and I know we became much tighter after that class.
(Anonymous Diary Entry from October, 2007)

"To teach is to touch a live forever." – Anonymous

I have been in education for 36 years. I firmly believe this to be a true statement. I also believe a good teacher is not in education for positive feedback and accolades from his/her students. As a teacher the statement needs to guide your actions – because you never really know how you are impacting your students, either in a positive way, or heaven forbid, in a negative way.

As a school librarian, my student time usually does not afford me the opportunity to really interact with students beyond their immediate academic needs in the library situation. Several years ago this changed. Back in the 2006-07 school year, we began a class called Academic Skills. The goal of the class was to give our general level freshmen a structured class to help them adjust academically and, in some cases, socially to being a high school student. I became involved with the class to help the students improve their reading and research skills. The scheduled teacher for the class was Anne Schober. That year began an interesting journey as we struggled to develop an academic program to meet the needs of the students. It was a struggle; every day brought a new challenge. We both realized early in the school year that before we could get the students to improve academically, we needed to challenge them to overcome the problems they faced outside the classroom.

During that year "To teach is to touch a live forever" had even more meaning to me; it almost became a mantra to get me through the year. I needed to tell myself that what little academic success the students had that year would hopefully translate to a better life as they matured into adults.

Within the next year, Anne was awarded the chance to learn the Freedom Writer methodology through the Freedom Writer Institute. That changed how Anne focused the students in the Academic Skills class. The new school year *began with academics coming second. The main focus for the first weeks of school was getting the students to believe in themselves. This culminated with the class completing the "Toast for Change."*

The Academic Skills class eventually became Communications. Communications became the English class for the lower level students from freshman to senior year. It became a project learning based class. I regret that during the next few years my responsibilities in the Library cut down on the time I could spend in the classroom with the Communications students.

If you can look at one group over another and pick which class was the most "successful" it would be the group who named themselves The Mix. From the first day of class freshmen year, this was an eclectic mix of students. By senior year the core group of students remaining in The Mix accepted the challenge to make a difference in the world. By accepting the challenge they made a difference in their own lives. Although I often had to look on and cheer from the sidelines, the students and their successes in seeing their challenge become a reality was an inspiration to me. The impact they had on the students at Kirkpatrick will stay with them forever. Hopefully it continues to spur them on to even greater accomplishments.

This brings me back to the beginning, "To teach is to touch a live forever." I was lucky, with The Mix. I saw their success first hand, and I knew I played a very small role in changing lives. Teachers must remember that most of the time we do not see the impact we have on the lives of our students. But either in small ways or larger ways you have touched the lives of your students, so strive to make it always a positive way.

Susan M. Martin
Librarian, Lancaster Catholic High School

Part Four
The Rest of the Story…

> "The most important lesson that I have learned is to trust God in every circumstance. Lots of times we go through different trials and following God's plan seems like it doesn't make any sense at all. God is always in control and he will never leave us."
>
> *Alyson Felix*

Having successful days in the classroom were many, but there were countless days when I just wanted to throw in the towel. I felt beaten, heartbroken and alone. Throughout my teaching career, I was humiliated by teachers who told their students that my class was not a "real" English class and they were not learning what they needed. When I told the office I would not be coming back the next year and gave them my official resignation, another teacher actually told her students that I was fired because I could not teach! On one occasion, I was being observed by someone in administration who stood in my doorway and asked, in front of my students, if I would be teaching today? Imagine my reaction! Members of my own department talked behind my back and considered me to be a poor teacher. The reason behind much of the criticism? I was playing music, my kids were talking, and there was no silence to be had unless there was a test. How could I possibly be teaching with that much racket going on in my room? I didn't even have a seating chart! The fact that others misunderstood my teaching methods is an understatement.

However, besides my observation, no teacher

ever bothered to come into my classroom to watch how I taught, the engagement my students held with each lesson, or the results that I achieved through my creative teaching style. Instead, they listened to students say that they loved my class because we played "games", such as the Line Game and Agree/Disagree, the literature we studied was actually relevant to their lives and the writing we accomplished was not the typical five paragraph essay... it was creative and it had purpose! I must not be a good teacher when my students are having fun because it is well known that you cannot learn when having fun!

After becoming a Freedom Writer teacher, I knew that I would be cheered on by some and neglected and shunned by others. I also knew that by opening myself to my students by teaching from my heart, there would be scars that would take a long time to heal. But, I knew the connections made would see me through even the darkest of times.

I was driving my daughter back to college in North Carolina when I received a phone call from one of my students. He wanted to let me know that his mother had "gone off the deep end" and accused me of having an affair with him. My heart jumped out of my skin and I was horrified, devastated, and terrified all wrapped up together.

This student had been kicked out of his house because of drug issues and was sent to live with his father. But, by living there, he would no longer be able to attend our school because of transportation issues. He was devastated and confused. I went in to talk with my principal and asked if I could bring him to school since he lived only five minutes away from my home. My principal agreed and, after I spoke with the student's father, we made the necessary arrangements of pick-up times, etc. Never, in a million years, would I have dreamed that something I did out of the kindness of my heart would be misconstrued as an attempt to have a secret affair!

I immediately called my husband who assured me that everything would be fine because this was ludicrous and, in no way, true. I then called my principal. When I told him about the phone call I received, he laughed! I felt myself relaxing. However, the harassment from this woman did not stop. Her accusations were becoming more ridiculous and my husband and I knew that it had to end. My reputation and teaching career were on the line.

We called a meeting with this woman, her ex-husband, the student, the principal and my husband after she was heard at a state wrestling tournament berating and accusing me in front of parents and students. We met for over an hour and after anger, tears, and disgust, my husband threatened a lawsuit if she did not stop the false accusations. I was told to not drive him to school anymore and to avoid contact with him as much as possible, which was quite hard to do since he was in two of my classes. But, I did as instructed. I kept my distance and prayed for him and his family every single day. Thankfully, we never heard from this woman again; however, the words she spewed would never go away.

I questioned my teaching so many times during that horrible ordeal, but I knew in a heartbeat that I would do it all over again if I had to. I did what was right in my heart, and I decided at that moment that teaching with my heart was what I was going to do, no matter how much it may hurt in the end.

Making connections can cause hurt, reach out anyway.

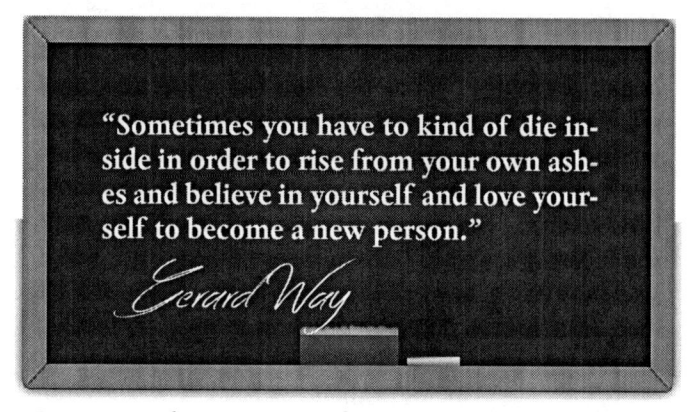

> "Sometimes you have to kind of die inside in order to rise from your own ashes and believe in yourself and love yourself to become a new person."
>
> *Gerard Way*

Hurt, pain, loss, anger, confusion are words that are often associated with teenagers from every walk of life. Sometimes, students become so wrapped up in a world where they feel they must act a certain way in order to keep friends that they begin to lose their sense of identity. This was the case with a talented, intelligent young man who sat in my class hiding behind a mask of alcohol and drugs.

Toward the end of his senior year, Adam Law did something that will never be forgotten. It was a typical day in class, writing and reflecting using a prompt I had assigned. That particular day I assigned the topic, "If you really knew me you would know…"

It was a popular prompt, and, as always, students either took them seriously or simply wrote about what was on their minds. This particular day you could have heard a pin drop. The students did not stop writing. And, as always, some shared their entries while others kept quietly to themselves. Toward the end of class, Adam waltzed up to my desk and threw the journal at me saying, "You are going to fucking love what I wrote". With those words, he quickly left with a smirk on his face.

My curiosity was up and instead of eating lunch

I began to read his entry. My heart dropped. Tears began forming. What the hell did I just read and what am I going to do? Adam had written that he was drunk as hell and then went on to say that he had been doing this for a long time and he didn't know how to stop. He was in trouble and maybe by writing it down it would help him sort things out. But, I was now in a place I didn't want to be. I couldn't let him drive home. I had to do something... so I called for the principal.

When the principal called me back, I was crying. I told him that I had a student who was in big trouble and before I told him his name, he needed to promise me that he would graduate with his class if he promised to get help. My principal agreed. Not many people would have done that, and because he did, this young man was given a chance.

I immediately went down to one of my best friends who I knew would be the perfect person for Adam to talk to and began to tell him the situation. Rich Hinnenkamp, the Athletic Director at Lancaster Catholic, has an amazing ability to relate to kids and promised me he would help him in any way he could.

Rich called Adam into his office and the next few hours were spent crying, talking, understanding and listening. As he opened up, the smell of booze quickly filled up the small room where we were meeting. I witnessed his demeanor changing. His shoulders began to slump, his eyes were searching. What started off as an innocent writing prompt led me into the soul of a troubled young man that needed help. That day was one that changed his life forever, but also changed mine. He was broken, and I failed to see it. But, through a simple writing exercise, two worlds collided and opened my eyes to the harsh realities hidden behind the smile of a lost soul.

Making connections can lead to secrets waiting to be discovered. Make time to explore.

When I was asked to write about any memorable experiences I had in class with Mrs. Schober, I knew exactly which experience that would be, but I did not quite know how to go about recalling it. And I still don't. At first I did not want to write it to explicitly simply because it was writing about this experience was why I was given an ultimatum while I was a senior at Lancaster Catholic High School. But the more I think about it, the more I realize there's no dodging it; I need to write it the way it happened.

Thursday, April 26, 2012 started out as a usual Thursday morning, at least for my buddy and me. We met up at Burger King by school at 7:30am, giving us enough time to grab a quick breakfast and take a few shots. And by a few, I mean about fifteen. It was not unusual for us to each drink a water bottle of vodka before school, sometimes three or even four days a week. It just made school that much more fun and interesting. And that Thursday started out fun and interesting just like I was hoping, until fifth period with Mrs. Schober.

Senior English was always a class I enjoyed, not for the English, but for my classmates and teacher. We always were learning something in a fun and exciting manner, often having little to do with English. That day was no exception. Instead of opening up our grammar books and highlighting the past participial phrases in ten sentences, we opened up our writer's notebooks and were given a prompt. Our writer's notebooks were our very own journals; what goes in them stays in them, unless of course you wish to share. The prompt for that Thursday was "What would you know about me if you really knew me?" Even before Mrs. Schober started explaining the prompt, I could already see people scribbling in their notebooks to get as many thoughts in as possible, as if this would be the last thing they ever write.

At first I did not have a clue as to what to write; I've always been a very open person, and I honestly had no secrets. I can keep others' secrets, but I have no "promise you won't tell anyone?" stories about myself. It wasn't until I heard anonymous examples from the earlier class that I decided what to write.

Mrs. Schober stood in the front of the class reading stories that were absolutely disheartening, disappointing, and borderline unbelievable. "If you really knew me, you would know I was born addicted to heroin because my mother was an addict when she was pregnant with me." "If you really knew me, you would know the reason I don't go to football and basketball games is because I work until midnight after school so I can pay my tuition and feed my little brother. My mom is on drugs and I haven't seen my dad in seven years." "If you really knew me, you would know I cry every night when I hear my mom screaming while my dad is punching her for not having dinner ready when he got home." WOW! These are people I go to school with. Not a public, inner city school. These are people that attend Lancaster Catholic High School, the preppy alternative for upper-middle class families to keep their children out of public school (and some for the religion aspect, too).

As I sat there terribly intoxicated, I too began to jot down my immediate thoughts before I would lose it and go onto another. I wrote not about "if you really knew Adam Law," but more about "Holy Schnikes, how do other people live these lives right in front of me? They have actual problems to deal with while I am a white kid from a two parent family, and the only troubles I have are because I, me, myself, nobody else but me, effed up smoking pot or coming up drunk at 4am." (And here's where it all went "wrong") "I'm even drunk as shit right now writing this." At the end of class, Mrs. Schober noted I was writing at a torrid pace, and asked if I would care to share it with her.

Not even thinking about that one line in there, I handed it over to her telling her she might find it "rather" interesting. Off to lunch I went.

It was the period after lunch when the assistant athletic director collected me from study hall, saying he needed help in his office. I did not think much of it until I walked in and Mrs. Schober was sitting there. I thought immediately that I was in trouble. It turns out, the assistant AD was formerly a drug and alcohol counselor and subsequently Mrs. Schober's best friend. The three of us sat and talked for a few minutes about what I had written before the principal and my father joined us. During that time we talked not so much about me being drunk, but about exactly what I wrote… how can such travesties be going on right around me? To avoid boring you with the details of my situation, I will sum it up by saying I received the choice of being expelled or remaining at Catholic under the conditions I admit I have a drinking problem and seek treatment for this problem. I spent the rest of the year and that summer going to an outpatient drug and alcohol rehabilitation program with other teens for fifteen hours a week.

My friends and people I tell this story to constantly tell me I am an idiot for sharing my notebook and confessing my insobriety with a __TEACHER!__ And while it is very easy to agree with them because I would not have gotten myself in that hole, I do not regret it for a second. I think that for some reason on that day, I was supposed to turn that notebook in. It was on that day, in that classroom, that I was truly opened up to the world and how people are truly individuals and unique. I knew everybody was different, but to me that meant they have different jobs, drive different cars, some have brothers, some have sisters. It never crossed my mind that when I see vicious stories on the news, I am actual among these people. I thought after school everybody went to their lessons, practices, part time jobs, or what have you, and then ate dinner with their family recapping the events of the day. Mrs. Schober's class taught me to give everybody a chance. Everybody has a story and it needs to be shared. That quiet girl might not just be quiet because she is "weird." She just might not know how to tell you she hasn't eaten in three days without feeling embarrassed. That boy by himself wants to be cool and popular and it's not his fault he doesn't know how to interact with you. He just doesn't have an Xbox or a TV at home; instead he gets beaten by his step-father after a long day at school. I was truly opened up to humanity in room 123, and I honestly can say that I take this with me every single day when I meet new people.

Even at my current job, two years removed from this incident, I still remember what I learned that day. On the surface, it is easy to call this guy a deadbeat nigger line cook with nothing going for him in his life. Often, that's exactly how other coworkers consider him. It wasn't until I offered him a ride home so he wouldn't have to walk two miles at one in the morning to his home. While in the car, he shared with me how he first murdered someone at thirteen as part of a gang initiation in Arkansas. He also never graduated high school, and spent five years of his life on the run for an attempted homicide charge. Pretty easy to see why he would be called a deadbeat nigger. But he also told me how he regrets these incidences and wishes they weren't a part of his life. But he knows they are and he cannot change it. Now he spends his life working fifty hours a week as a line cook because nobody wants to hire a felon for a decent job. He saves his paychecks mainly for two things: paying college tuition at HACC and so that he will be able to afford a decent ring for his girlfriend by Christmas. She told him she doesn't need one, but he says that's all the more reason to get it for her. He told me she did everything to help him straighten his life out and he loves her more than anything and wants her to be his wife for the rest of his life, and he wants to be a "real man" and get down on one knee and give her a ring that will sweep her off her feet. He does all this as an overworked black line cook at a local diner. He is as real a person as you will ever meet and I wouldn't have known that if I didn't take the time to get to know him. And I surely wouldn't have taken the time to get to know him if I hadn't learned that valuable life lesson in room 123 with Mrs. Schober.

Adam Law, Student

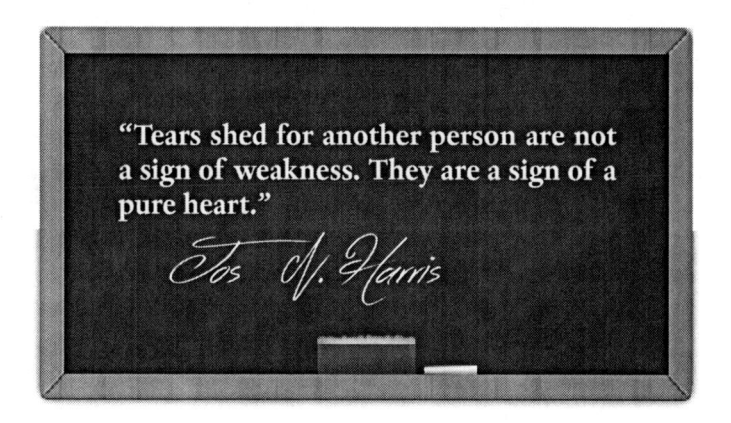

> "Tears shed for another person are not a sign of weakness. They are a sign of a pure heart."
>
> *Jos N. Harris*

Sometimes, the most tragic of events can cause one to wonder is it really worth getting to know your students only to lose them in the end? The answer is "Yes!" I will never forget the first time I lost a student due to violence. Cornell "Young EZ" Stewart was one of the most talented and warm people I ever had the pleasure of teaching and knowing. When I first met Cornell, he was a freshman in high school who loved being the center of attention, which sometimes got him into a bit of trouble. We were at an assembly, albeit it was very boring and the students were stuck in a hot gymnasium with a speaker who was monotone at best, but Cornell did not stop talking. I had to send him to the office, and he was not happy.

The next time I met him, he was a senior and a student in my College Composition and Speech class. We took our time getting to know each other and, by the end of the first quarter, I had gained Cornell's trust and respect. We formed a strong bond where he would share his rap music with me and I would help him with research papers and organization. His music was powerful. He rapped of his troubles, his struggles, his passions, his thoughts, his worries, and his life. I was overwhelmed by his words. When he spoke of racism still evident in the world, and in our school, his truthfulness and passion were overwhelming. When he wrote of the pain of a broken family, my heart ached for him. His talent was so powerful that even while sitting in class the songs and beats would never cease. It was sad to see him graduate, but the future was bright for him; I knew that someday he would become the star he always wanted to be.

May 8, 2010, Cornell "Young EZ", was taken from this world while doing what he loved best... rapping. Cornell was at a club, performing, when another rapper approached ready to start a fight with one of EZ's friends. Cornell went out back, after he finished his set, to take a break. As he walked out the back door, one shot rang out and struck Cornell in the head. He never regained consciousness. He was taken to the hospital and was quickly surrounded by family and friends. When I heard what happened, my husband and I headed to the hospital to see him.

The vision of Cornell, lying lifeless in the white sterility of the hospital room, will never leave my mind. His head had swelled to twice its normal size. This was not my Cornell. I held his hand, cried with his mother, and left his room knowing I would never see him again.

I went home that night and held my own children closer than ever before and realized that this world would never be the same. We lost a talented and loved rapper that would never get the chance to see his dreams come true.

Before his funeral, I went back to my classroom to find what I knew would be a comfort to his family. Every day in class, I asked my students to write.

It didn't have to be anything special, just something that was on their mind, a question they had, an experience they wanted to remember. Cornell wrote songs. When he graduated, I asked if I could keep his music and he, with his beautiful smile, said "Of course". I knew that his family would take solace in knowing that his words would never die.

When it was time for the visitation, I held the notebook tightly in my hand, almost scared to let this memory of Cornell leave my grasp. When I approached his mother, I gave her a hug, looked her in the eyes and said, "I want you to have this. These are Cornell's words, his music, and his life. He wrote this when he was a senior in my English class and I think it is meant for you to have them." Her tears expressed her thanks and my tears expressed my sadness for her loss. We embraced for what seemed like hours and I left her side, glanced at Cornell one last time, and walked away with memories of Cornell forever engraved on my heart and the beat of his life etched in my soul. Cornell, my rapping angel.

I wish I could say that Cornell was the only student I have lost, but it is not. My last year in the classroom was "book-ended" with the passing of two students who were in my College Composition class. Both were students in the same period. Both were quiet, honest, respectful, mature, and beautiful souls. Both left a vacancy in my heart and the class of 2013. Both were taken too soon.

Kevin Wolgemuth loved being outside, going to his families cabin, and Notre Dame Football. He played basketball, video games, and lived in a small, tight knit community. He died when a tree that was being cut down at their cabin came crashing down on him. His classmates were heartbroken. His seat sat vacant for the remainder of the year, and his loss is still felt today. Kevin, my Notre Dame fighting angel.

Jocelynne Reisinger loved her brothers, sunflowers, and had the best friends you could imagine. Her smile was contagious and her writing was intensely moving and advanced. She was driving home from her boyfriend's house, in a hurry to meet her curfew, lost control of her car, and died on impact. She had graduated only one week prior to her accident. Her death shook the class of 2013 to its very core. Jocelynne, my smiling sunflower angel.

Both of these students were members of the last class I would ever teach and their passing still haunts me. How can two young lives be taken so suddenly? My career at Lancaster Catholic began with the death of a teacher and ended with the deaths of two students.

Making connections can bring pain, heartache, and hurt. Love anyway.

*   *   *

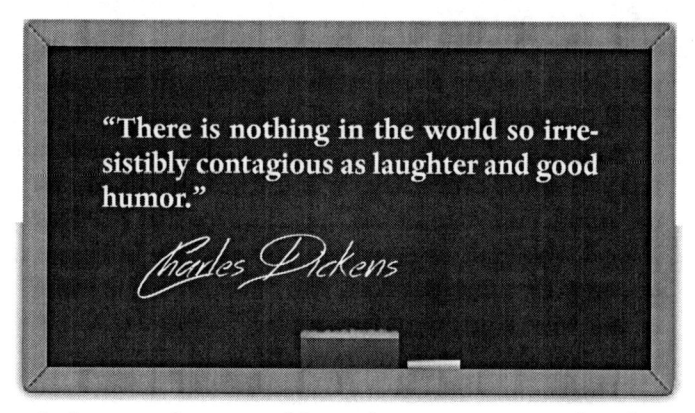

> "There is nothing in the world so irresistibly contagious as laughter and good humor."
>
> *Charles Dickens*

In between the tears of loss, there were many laughs. I remember when a student asked if he could ask a girl to the prom during my class. I, of course, said yes! The next day, he came in dressed in a gorilla outfit and hid in my closet until the intended target of his affection entered the room. As I began class, he jumped out of the closet, traveled morosely toward the unknowing young lady and said, "I will go bananas if you don't go to prom with me!" She, of course, said yes. How could you not when a 6'8" gorilla pines for your attention?

One moment I will never forget was when I completely embarrassed myself in front of my students, which was not a rare occurrence. I loved keeping candy on my desk for the kids to have whenever they chose. However, there came a day, or two, when the candy dish was left empty. I had not been to the store in a few days and the kids were missing their sweets. When one class of seniors walked in, many asked when I was going to get more candy.

Without hesitation, I simply said, "I will be getting some soon because I am having BJ withdrawal".

The laughter could be heard down the hall and I had no idea why they were laughing.

Bobby Checchia, a student I have known since he was born, looked at me with a goofy grin and said, "Did you really just say that?"

And then it hit me! My face turned the beetest red you could ever imagine and I was mortified. In my mind, everyone should have known that BJ's was a local wholesale store where you can buy in bigger quantity for a cheaper cost. However, sitting in front of me were a group of teenagers. To this day, those infamous words have followed me from year to year.

Throughout the years, laughter was a constant sound emanating from room 123. From dancing, jokes, games and plenty of April Fools pranks that were not confined to one day, laughter proved to brighten the darkest days and lift the saddest of spirits. I had a group of students try to teach me how to "Dougie", while another group of students had hijacked my computer and fixed it so that they could advance my slides while giving a lecture. Laughter brought us together, unifying class after class, one smile and chuckle at a time.

Sometimes a smile is the only connection needed to change a life.

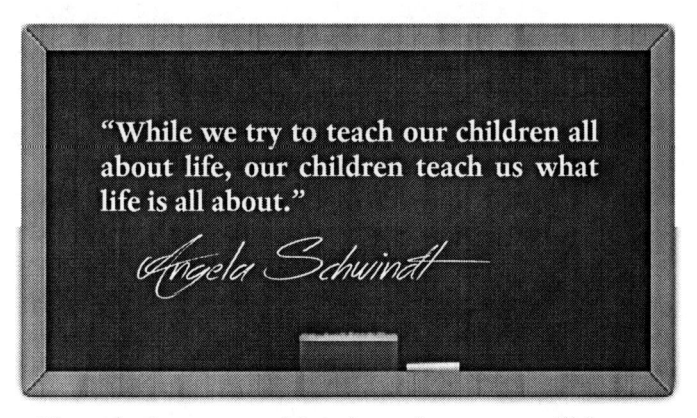

> "While we try to teach our children all about life, our children teach us what life is all about."
>
> *Angela Schwindt*

Through the tears and laughter, there were still lessons to be taught and learned. While studying the Holocaust, I helped my students to question their own belief systems and morals. While studying *The Things They Carried*, I challenged them to be mindful of veterans and their stories. While discovering our service project for the year, I reminded them that there are people who deserve our efforts and support. But, planning these lessons did not come easily. To make the lessons relevant and engaging, I had to do a lot of work at home.

Researching supplements to enhance the literature studied, discovering videos to enrich author study, searching for writing prompts that would enlighten my students, and finding guest speakers to bring reality to what we were studying was more than a brief undertaking. Every day after school you would find me in the same spot on my couch in the family room with my computer on my lap and piles of papers on my side, waiting to be graded. The outline of my backside is still imprinted in the same spot, and it makes me queasy when I see it. Having between 120 and 160 students a year, as well as four to five preps every day, did not allow for me to do anything more than to grade, plan and begin again.

I loved teaching at Lancaster Catholic for many reasons. It was my alma mater where I learned from the most passionate of teachers and where I grew from a teenager into an adult. I also adored the fact that I would be able to teach my own children. While some may struggle with that idea, I embraced it. I relished the idea of being able to see my children every day.

I was nervous the first time my daughter, Michelle, walked into my classroom, but then it became calming. I knew that within the sea of hormonal eyes, one set of them belonged to my daughter and that made me relax. However, I never thought of what my children had to endure by having their mom as a teacher in a school where they were learning to be themselves.

I remember hearing students ask my children if there was going to be a pop quiz, a test, or if I would change a due date for a project, but it never dawned on me the amount of pressure they were under as my children. They had to learn to share me with hundreds of other kids and sometimes that proved to be stressful for all of us.

When reflecting on my teaching career at Lancaster Catholic, having my own children as my students is a blessing of which I will forever be grateful. At home, I could see they were growing and maturing, but in the school environment I witnessed their transformation into adulthood. I was a part of their questioning, their yearning for understanding, and I was responsible for making sure that they were ready to embark on their next chapter in life, moments that I would have never witnessed if I had not been their teacher.

My family is my foundation, my connecting piece to life and all its wonders. I am blessed.

She taught me to walk. She taught me my manners. She taught me pretty much everything I know about life. And I'm still learning from her today...whether I like it or not! My mom was my first teacher, my forever teacher... and yes, even my high school English teacher.

It was the second semester of my junior year in high school. I had a group of good friends, did well in my classes and was beginning to think about college. My English teacher was having a baby and went on "permanent maternity leave" at Christmas. Since the first day of school, we all knew we would be getting a new teacher when we came back in January...at the time, I had no idea that person would be my mom.

Before I go on, let me just put it out there that I love my mom to death. Absolutely, truly and unconditionally love her. She's a best friend and my hero. I admire her, look up to her and pray every day that she can see in herself what everyone else sees in her...true beauty.

Now, with that being said, I can go on (for reasons you'll see why in a few seconds). When I got the news that my mom would be my teacher, I was happy...For her that is. She always wanted to teach at Lancaster Catholic, her alma mater, and this was the perfect opportunity for her. She was excited and anxious and ready to begin this new journey. I, on the other hand, was quite hesitant....but who was I to get in the way of my mom fulfilling her dreams?

For example, when I had writing assignments for other classes and teachers, I never showed them to my mom before handing them in. I hated having to show my writing to anyone close to me, especially my mom. I'm not sure if I was scared of her feedback or if I just wasn't confident enough in my own writing, but now I was going to be forced to have her read it. And grade it. And critique it.

I also knew that everyone would loooooove her. Everyone who came in contact with her already did and I knew my fellow peers would share the same sentiment. There's a running joke in my family that whenever we go out in public and see one of her students, it's always "Mrs. Schober! Mrs. Schober!" Yep, everyone loves my mom.

So what's wrong with that? Absolutely nothing. I'm honored to have such a loveable and amazing mom, I really am. But as the second semester of my junior year began, all of my anxieties and predictions were falling right into place.

First, I never knew what to call my mom in school: "Mom," "Mrs. Schober," "Hey you." It was so awkward for me that I don't think I called her anything in class. I simply raised my hand and waited to be called on. Then came the writing assignments. I cringed every time I handed my paper over to her. And what was worse was when she sat at home grading it. I couldn't look her in the eyes, let alone be in the same room as her when I knew mine was on the top of her pile. It was torture.

And right on cue came all of the expected questions: "Did you get an A because your mom's the teacher?" "Does she help you at home with your homework?" "Do you get to look at the questions before a test?" No, no and no! I was a hard working student and earned my A's myself but now, not only did I have to prove myself in the classroom, I had to prove my smarts to my peers so they would stop nagging me about it.

Finally, my biggest "fear" was becoming a reality, as well. Just as I predicted, everyone fell in love with my mom. She was an amazing teacher and was able to engage her students in "Wuthering Heights" and Shakespeare. I knew I was in trouble when the normal "Hey Miki's!" in the hallways were replaced with "Hey Miki, your mom is AWESOME" and "Hey, how's your mom doing?" From that point on, I was no longer just Miki Schober, I was Mrs. Schober's daughter.

Again, let me refer back to my third paragraph. I love my mom and can't help but be proud when I hear praises about her. But, when you are 16 years old and still trying to establish your identity and place in high school, this didn't help. So needless to say, I "silently" rolled my eyes anytime I was asked how my mom was doing before myself. Along those same lines, I did feel a tinge of jealousy, too. Now I had to share my mom with all of her other students and getting used to that idea was hard.

Cut ahead ten years later and I still feel a little bitter about my experience with mom as my teacher. Not because of what I mentioned above (I'm so over that!) but because I got jipped. Yes, jipped. I still learned a heck of a lot in class but in all honesty, it was your standard, run of the mill, high school English class. You see, it wasn't until recently that my mom developed a new teaching style and method, and lucky for my brother and his classmates, they were able to experience it firsthand. If you ask my brother, he will tell you he had the best high school experience with my mom as his teacher. So unfair.

But despite all of my petty complaints ten years ago, I do admit that I wouldn't trade having my mom as a teacher for anything. I absolutely loved having her with me every day and loved knowing she was there if I needed her. I loved that everyone loved her, and still do. I love that I still get to learn from her and appreciate everything she has taught me.

And what I love even more is that I get to call her "mom." I am so unbelievably proud of what she has accomplished and can't wait to see what she does next! She is a wonderful person, teacher and mom and lucky for you, you get to have this little piece of her, as well.

Michelle Schober, Daughter and Student

Mrs. Mom

There were many names I was referred to as in all of my years of schooling, including my current college years. Some were, but are not limited to, "teacher's pet", "goodie-two-shoes", "smart ass", "perfect student", "smartest kid in class", and I could go on for days. But only one year out of my 14 years of school was I ever referred to as "The teacher's son". Many people aren't sure what it would be like to have their mom or dad as their teacher; I know I wasn't sure what it was going to be like, either. My sister, Michelle, was the first to have her; in fact she was one of the first students ever at Lancaster Catholic to have her. She thought it was pretty awkward. Joey, my other sister, thought it was so-so. I was completely different.

The summer going into senior year, I knew I was going to have my mom as my English and Speech teacher. Yep, twice a day. Out of all her students that year, you can bet your bottom dollar that I was the most excited. I was already involved in so many clubs with her, why not tack on two classes (we pretty much ran the school). My mom and I checked out the class rosters, and sure enough half the class was full of my best friends; friends that my mom cooked for, friends that my mom drank in front of, and friends that crashed at our house almost every weekend. We both knew that not only was this class going to be fun, but we were never going to get anything accomplished. We were both wrong.

Each student walked out of that classroom each day learning something new about his or her own self. I didn't think that was going to happen, but I knew my mom had it planned all along. We spent so much time discovering who we were and then we wrote about it. Because of my mom, us big, bad seniors dug deep into our minds and wrote about life experiences. Some were hilarious, some scary, and some life changing. If it wasn't for her, so many people *might not have never told a specific story about their life, but they knew that with Mrs. Schober standing right by their side, they could do anything because she filled them with the courage and bravery to do something we wouldn't normally do. I was included in that.*

A common question to us kids who have their parent as a teacher is, "What do you call them?" I wasn't sure how that was going to play out at the beginning of my senior year. As always, I managed to adjust quickly. If I ever needed her or was calling out in class, I would just shout, "Ma!!!" I know she loved it. Another common question we receive is, "Do you get away with a lot of stuff?" To answer this question with the utmost respect, yes, if you play your cards right. My mom was a sucker to me and the rest of the gang, but especially me. Many times I would walk into class and say "Mom, we are all so tired and we have so much other stuff to do, can we please push this paper back a few days?" She would smile, laugh, and dive right into my puppy dog eyes. She would order a class vote to see who all agreed. Eleven times out of ten it was unanimous. I wasn't taking advantage of her, I was, like I said, playing my cards right.

Without a doubt, it was the best class I ever took in high school and she was, without a doubt, the best teacher in that high school. She wasn't a hard teacher or a test teacher, and no that's not what made her the best. She was a life teacher who made going to class every single day fun, exciting, and surprising. I could have taken AP English my senior year but, instead, I dropped down to College Prep to take my mom's class because I knew that I was going to get more than just an English grade at the end of the year. I walked out of that class with a sense of who I was. I walked out of that class with the courage to tackle the world. I walked out of that class knowing that so many people have so many different hardships in their lives. I walked out of that class knowing that I will always have a teacher to be by my side and help me in any time of need. Lucky for me that teacher was also my mom.

At home, she was mom, at school she was still mom, the only difference is at school I had many more brothers and sisters. That's how my mom was; she took each and every one of her students and looked at them as her child. Words cannot express what that meant to all my classmates and me. Knowing that we all had someone to hug and vent to was comforting. She has gotten so many people through their hardest points in their life, including me. I will never be able to thank her enough for what she has done for me, and I don't think she quite understands the capacity behind that. She has changed so many lives, especially mine, and I admire her more than anyone. Her teaching skills and mentality were unlike any other; they brought out only the good in people and made us discover ourselves. A lot of teachers are incapable of this, but she excelled.

I am so lucky to have Mrs. Schober as my mom. She has accomplished so much in her life and I am honored to be her son. She has been my rock in times of need, my biggest fan, my teacher, my motivator, and my role model. What my mom has done for me as a student, but more importantly as a person, is something I can't even put into words and I know this is the same case for many of her other students. There aren't many teachers out there with students who can say these kinds of words about them. I am not just saying these things because I am her son, I am saying these things because they are the absolute truth. Without her, I don't know where I would be in my life and I don't want to think about it. This small piece of writing will never be good enough to justify what she has done for me, but it is a start. I love you mom, and I am so proud of what you have accomplished, the person you are, and the person you made me. Thank you, Mrs. Mom.

Stephen Schober, Son and Student

> "No, this is not the beginning of a new chapter in my life; this is the beginning of a new book! That first book is already closed, ended, and tossed into the seas; this new book is newly opened, has just begun! Look, it is the first page! And it is a beautiful one!"
>
> — *C. JoyBell C.*

My new life is just beginning and the world is now my classroom. If I could go back in time, would I change anything? Absolutely not. Every moment, good or bad, has created who I am today. Because of these experiences, I have learned more than I ever thought possible. And that is why I chose to write this book.

Making connections, taking the time to talk to a person you are sitting next to on the bus or a student in your own classroom, can be life changing. Knowing that each person has a story and taking the time to learn that story can open your eyes to a new world.

Erin Gruwell taught me to respect each person I meet and to take the time to learn the stories that surround my students. She taught me to believe in myself as a person, educator, and cheerleader for the at-risk youth that God graciously placed in my care, and the college bound students that needed guidance. She taught me to teach with my heart.

And, I succeeded. Through the tears, hiccups, laughs and screams, I know that I positively affected at least ONE student and that is all that matters. Because, as Ralph Waldo Emerson once said, "To know even one life has breathed easier because you have lived, this is to have succeeded."

Part Five
Stories Yet to Be Told

> "When you study great teachers... you will learn much more from their caring and hard work than from their style."
>
> *William Glasser*

While my life in Room 123 has come to an end, there are many, many heroes that are still fighting battles today. Amidst the budget cuts, new government standards, and testing that never seems to end, teachers are in a thankless profession. And yet, they continue to teach. I applaud them and I know that their students are better people because they have been a part of their life and education.

Teaching with your heart can be hard on your emotional soul. As the barriers are torn down and teachers become real with their students, vulnerability is at stake. Going through education classes, I was often told, "Never smile before Christmas" and "Do not listen to excuses from your students". And yet, I DID smile before Christmas and I DID listen to excuses. That is what made me the teacher I was.

While my stories from the classroom are complete, there are others who are just beginning. My middle daughter, JoAnne, is just beginning her life in the classroom and witnessing her excitement, mixed with her exhaustion, takes me back to my very first day in the classroom. Seeing her come home with a smile on her face when she recounts mastering long division with her students, makes me proud. Having her walk through the door with a somber heart as she recalls the turmoil of one of her students whose father was just put in jail, makes me realize that she is going to be one hell of a good teacher because already she is learning to teach with her heart. She is making connections.

Making connections with others will forever change your life.

"All that I am or hope to be, I owe to my mother." *I am one of the very few women who can honestly look at their mother, and call them their best friend. I constantly question how one woman can be so full of love and deep, true beauty. I mean, how is that possible??? How can one individual make such a HUGE difference in the lives of their students? How can one individual inspire a teenager so lost in depression and their own gloomy, dark world? How can one individual make a student who has zero confidence believe that they are the change this world needs? I don't know if I will ever be able to answer those questions. But if I had to answer, I would say only a person with so much passion in their heart, they can't hold it in, can make that big of a difference. That person is my mom.*

I always knew I wanted to be a teacher. From the early days of playing "school" with my stuffed animals and my miniature chalkboard, I was destined to be a teacher. However, the older I got, I wasn't exactly sure that was my calling. I walked off the "teacher road" for a bit and entered the psychology world. Man oh man, what was I thinking?? Clearly, I was not meant to be a psychology major. What in the world did God want me to do? During this time in my life, my mom was ROCKING the education world. Her students, The Mix, were my sisters and brothers. These kids were incredible. They were the strongest, funniest, down-to-earth high school kids out there. They were REAL! And they have gone through so much in their life at such a young age. They were as people call "at risk" youth with crappy lives. I like to think of them as the "at risk to change the world" youth. And boy did they make the world rumble.

It wasn't just The Mix that my mom impacted. My mother impacted every single child that stepped foot in her classroom. Room 123 was the room of change. I knew how big an impact she was making solely by looking at the face of her students and seeing her body language at the end of day. She came home totally exhausted, yet, she still managed to raise a family of three, do laundry, cook dinner, and be a mom.

The Mix and my mom influenced me to walk back into the teacher world. In December of 2012, I earned my Bachelor's degree in Elementary Education. The Mix, and that dynamite woman (my mom) were the calling that I needed. Now, I am in my first year of teaching and although there are its ups and downs, the teaching profession is truly beautiful. These past five months have been the most humbling and eye-opening experience. Teaching is an art and my mom is my constant encouragement. There is a long road of teaching ahead, but I know that I have the best teacher. With my mom as my mentor, I am ready to change my students and future students, lives.

My mom is my inspiration. She made me realize that I NEEDED to teach. Just by witnessing how big of a change she was making, I knew I needed to follow in her footsteps. God, I can only hope I make half the difference in my student's lives that she has created. My mom, Mrs. Schober, created this tunnel of hope for her students. She created a tunnel that allowed her students to reach out and grab their dreams. She gave them hope. She gave them love. She gave them her entire self. She believed in them and told them, "YES, YOU CAN!" I, as well as many educators, aspire to be the type of teacher Anne Schober was, and still is. Honestly, how lucky am I to call her mine? As I go forth in my teaching career, I would be selfish not to my credit my mom for my successes. After all, she is my inspiration. She is a teacher who rocks the world.

The two biggest and most important things my mom has taught me in regards to teaching is this: First, Every student has a story. Be patient and Listen. Secondly, BELIEVE. Believe in your students, believe in yourself, and believe in change. YOU can be the change the world needs….just believe.

As Henry Adams once stated, "A teacher affects eternity: he can never tell where his influence stops." Mom, your influence in my life and my teaching career is never ending. I can only hope to be half the woman you are. You are unstoppable.

JoAnne Schober, Daughter, Student and Teacher

Moments of Anne, A Mohole Filled With Love

Anne Schober is the kindest redhead the world has ever known. Well, at the very least, my world. Her perpetual spirit and resilience has left an impression on many students' hearts and minds throughout her teaching career. She has created hope and love in places no one else thought was possible, or even practical. In addition to her passion inside the classroom, she has an unusual talent of making others happy. As a current high school teacher, it is a talent I wish I had paid more attention to.

Anne had created relationships with her students that enabled her to not only inspire, but also empower each student that has sat in her classroom. Her grounded approach and compassionate interaction with us helped to create an environment unlike anything secondary education had ever seen. But the one aspect of Anne I had never seen in school before, or since, was her ability to connect with students during one-on-one conversations; it was like the rest of the world disappeared and she was devoted to you and only you in that moment.

During these moments, Anne was able to change a student's life through just a touch of love, joy, sympathy, strength, or even humor. For me, one of the most powerful moments of Anne's unending impact in my life came when we discovered our nicknames for each other.

It was a dreary morning in March when Anne and I found our nicknames. Little did I know that on this rainy Thursday, these silly nicknames would become a source of strength, comfort, and joy for the next six years, and probably many more years to come.

I was in the library trying to study and stay awake during 1st period study hall when Anne came in with her Study Skills students to use the computers. The librarian, Miss Martin, was going to give them a lesson on how to use *a database to find information. I was only half listening to her instructions for the other students do a search. My attention was drawn to the lesson when a student tried to say the answer to a question and stumbled across the odd word on her screen.*

"Mohole, yes! A Mohole is essentially a deep hole to the next layer of Earth," Miss Martin had explained. As the students and I giggled at the funny word, Anne had "B lined" it straight over to my table at the other end of the library with a beaming smile on her face and said "You're such a Mohole! That's your name now!" My nickname until this point in school was just "Mo"- a name with very little meaning to me, so I instantly accepted this new one even if Anne was going to be the only one using it.

As we both burst out laughing and she returned to her students, I didn't realize how monumental that second of time would become in my life. Through the rest of my tears, laughs, mishaps, memories, broken smiles, kind words, and bruises of high school, college, and professional career, this moment is one that I hold the tightest. It was a moment when Anne's gift of happiness had passed into my heart; and it was my responsibility to kindle this happiness so I could look to it again when I needed it… and I would need it, again and again over the next six years. Each time I reread a letter, email, or inscription from Anne with this nickname, I was brought back to that moment in time when a feeling of happiness filled me up.

In a judgmental, vigilant, and competitive high school society, the need to feel happy and accepted becomes just as vital as breathing and walking to class on time. This contagious aura was the most valuable gift Anne bestowed upon me- and has become my lethal weapon against negativity and feelings of worthlessness in my own high school classroom. I try to replicate Anne's moments with my own students, and I know that I am making a difference when they remember the same special feeling I did when I was in their shoes. That is the real success, isn't it? When you pass the torch to the next generation and they continue the march. These tiny, precious moments that I hold in my heart will also fill another's and relay the same happiness.

Anne and I are changing the world- one moment at a time.

Monica Barnett, Student and Teacher

JoAnne and Monica are just two of many teachers who are creating memories every single day and changing lives. Every day there is a teacher who changes a life. Every day there is a student who wouldn't be here if that one teacher did not take the time to learn their story. Every day there are good things happening in the classroom, and I want to hear about them!

What was the best lesson you have taught? What impact did that lesson have on you? Your students? What was that one moment when all you wanted to do was cry? What was the funniest thing that happened to you in your classroom? As a student, what teacher stood out to you and why? What teacher made your life better because of something that happened in their classroom? As a parent, what one teacher impacted your son and/or daughter and why?

In this world of teachers making the front page news because of negative actions, it is time to spread the good news of teachers making a difference in the lives of students every day. It is time to be proud of the educational profession. It is time to embrace the beautiful moments that happen every day in classrooms around the world. It is time to celebrate! Because right now a student is looking to their teacher to guide them, accept them, nurture them and be there for them. And one day, that student could be a teacher that changes the world… and it all began with a teacher who taught with their heart. It all began because one teacher made a connection with one student. It all began because someone cared.

Submit your stories to: Anne Schober at anne-schober@comcast.net Please include your name, address, phone and email with your submission.

*"People are unreasonable, illogical, and self-centered.
Love them anyway.*

*If you do good, people may accuse you of selfish motives.
Do good anyway.*

*If you are successful, you may win false friends and true enemies.
Succeed anyway.*

*The good you do today may be forgotten tomorrow.
Do good anyway.*

*Honesty and transparency make you vulnerable.
Be honest and transparent anyway.*

*What you spend years building may be destroyed overnight.
Build anyway.*

*People who really want help may attack you if you help them.
Help them anyway.*

*Give the world the best you have and you may get hurt.
Give the world your best anyway."*

~

Mother Teresa